THE LITTLE BOOK OF
MINI

Written by **Brian Laban**

THE LITTLE BOOK OF
MINI

This edition first published in the UK in 2005
By Green Umbrella Publishing

© Green Umbrella Publishing 2009

Publishers Jules Gammond and Vanessa Gardner

Printed and bound in the UK

ISBN 978-1-906635-74-9

Contents

Introduction

FEW PEOPLE COULD HAVE KNOWN it at the time, but after 26 August 1959 the motoring world would change dramatically, in fact in the long term it would never really be the same again. 26 August 1959 was also the day when the traditional notion of the small car was turned on its ears, and when the layout that now dominates mass-production car design was first thrust into the mainstream. Because 26 August 1959 was Mini Day – the day on which one of the most significant, successful and best loved cars in motoring history was first introduced to the public.

It was a very different kind of car indeed, and looking back at it, a very brave one. By any standards it was genuinely small (on the outside at least), it was mechanically way different from the late 1950s norm, and it had a look like no other car on the road – a look that was all about function and had very little to do with fashion. Incredibly, though, one of the first leaps towards this little car's massive future success was that it would very soon become a fashion icon. And perhaps equally unlikely for a car that was launched with an 848cc engine and just 34bhp, it would become a sporting legend, too –

so strong that one of the most prestigious car makers in the world, BMW, took the reins and in 2000 turned the Mini into the MINI – a totally new second generation unmistakably drawing on the spirit of the first. And just as in 1959, it took the motoring world by storm.

In between, the original Mini - far from standing still as a superficial glance at its almost unchanging looks might suggest - had actually gone though literally thousands of improvements and dozens of widely differing models. There were booted Rileys and

ABOVE From the start, the Mini has been a favourite for motorsport

OPPOSITE The original Mini remained fundamentally unchanged throughout its life. This is a 1965 example

its giant-killing performances in racing and rallying completely overturning yet another motoring convention.

But perhaps most unlikely of all in an industry where change is the life blood, the Mini in almost precisely its original shape survived for more than forty years, and at the end of those four decades the concept and image were still

ABOVE The Mini has starred in countless films and TV shows. This is the car Rowan Atkinson drove as Mr Bean

It became a film and television star, in roles from The Italian Job to Mr Bean. It had become a genuine sports car alternative for hundreds of thousands of enthusiasts who either bought their Mini performance off the shelf with the various Cooper and Cooper S variants, or bought the basic car then bolted the excitement on later. And that coincidentally created a whole new industry for aftermarket tuning, body-kit and 'car improvement' specialists. Its creator insisted that he never intended it as a sporting car, but the Mini won dozens of major rallies including three victories in the great days of the Monte Carlo Rally, and it won the European Rally Championship outright. On the circuits it won the European Touring Car Championship outright, against far bigger and more powerful opposition, it won the British Saloon Car Championship outright – the final time in 1979, an incredible twenty years after the car's first appearance. In fact over the years it has won

Wolseleys, half-timbered estates, vans, pickups, convertibles and the Moke. The Mini had sold more or less around the world (with the notable exception of never conquering America), and before the very last example of the original Mini rolled off the production lines at Longbridge, near Oxford, in October 2000, it had sold almost five and a half million copies. It had become the first-car of choice for whole generations of cash-conscious young and new drivers, a car for families, and a car for celebrities, even for royalty.

literally thousands of events in every branch of motor sport from driving tests to hillclimbs, rallies to races, and at club level at least, original Minis were still winning long after the new generation MINI had been launched (and started its own sporting career).

But what the Mini won most of all was a kind of affection and iconic reputation that was way out of proportion to its diminutive size. And that's what makes the story of the Mini (and the MINI) one of the most fascinating in the whole history of motoring.

BELOW An impressive formation of MINI Ones, soon after the new car was launched in 2001

Chapter 1

The Seeds

NOW SPOOL BACK FOR A MOMENT to August 1959 and consider the world that the original Mini was born into – a world very different indeed from that which would welcome the second generation MINI, 42 years later. In Britain the year had started badly for motoring enthusiasts when newly crowned British World Champion racing driver Mike Hawthorn was killed in a road accident in Surrey in January. The hovercraft was the cutting edge of invention, and rock and roll was still in its infancy. Harold MacMillan was Prime Minister, and about to be re-elected as Britain enjoyed a generally affluent end to a decade that had had enough international unrest to create the need for a car like the Mini in the first place.

By the mid-1950s, when first thoughts for a car like the Mini were hatched, World War II, which had only ended in 1945, was still a relatively recent memory, and Britain's motor industry (which at the time was a far more important part of the country's industrial make-up than it is now) was only just getting properly back into its stride. For some time immediately after the war there had been no genuinely new cars, only rehashes of pre-war ones, because there simply wasn't the money or the resources to start from scratch. You also had to have government authorisation to buy one, and if you did it could cost you around twice what an

1950. By which time, the effects of the World War were fading, but the problems of Korea and Japan, the tensions between the USA, Russia and China, and the 'Cold War' threat of the atomic bomb were all never far from people's minds, even in Britain.

That said, Britain in the early years of the 1950s was pretty upbeat, and reasonably well off. In 1951 the Festival of Britain showcased our technical and cultural strengths, and in 1952 the launch of the Comet, the world's first commercial jet airliner, showed that it wasn't all just froth. There was a new, younger feeling in everyday life, too. A young queen was crowned in 1953, and

OPPOSITE With Queen Elizabeth II newly crowned, Britain was in an upbeat mood in the 1950s

BELOW De Havilland Comet, the world's first jet airliner, showcased Britain's technological prowess in the postwar years

essentially identical car had cost before the war – including a tax bill of two thirds the basic cost of the car. And, on government orders, much of what was being built was strictly for export only anyway, to earn the money to pay for the imported raw materials to put British industry back on its feet. Even for those who could buy a car, either a 'new' one or a second-hand one, necessities like tyres and fuel were still in short supply – and in fact petrol rationing, introduced early in the war, wouldn't actually be scrapped until May

an entirely new species, the teenager, began to make life a bit more exciting and a lot less staid. They even had a reasonable amount of money to spend as Britain found its way again, and gradually, as postwar restrictions lifted, there were things to spend it on.

In the car world, even that was getting better – well, marginally better. The early years of the 1950s had seen the market for new cars starting to grow again, and the main manufacturers getting increasingly aggressive about chasing sales. So in 1953 the £390 Ford Popular (admittedly still in a prewar

shape and very basic indeed) was the cheapest four-cylinder car in the world. In the mid 1950s you could also have the homegrown Austin A30 for £475, the Morris Minor for £529 or the Standard 8 for £481, and they were all, in the broad sense, small cars.

Even while the country and the wider world were recovering, though, a new problem was emerging that would have major implications for the motor industry – and these political developments were the single most significant trigger to the start of the Mini story.

Only months after petrol rationing had officially ended for British motorists in the early summer of 1950, a situation began to emerge which would bring an entirely new threat to fuel supplies from the middle east. In November 1950 King Farouk of Egypt demanded that British troops should withdraw totally and immediately from the Suez Canal Zone that they had occupied and protected since the end of the war. Britain refused, officially because the Zone was part of its defence programme, more practically because the Canal was the only way that oil from the Arab oilfields could reach Europe without going halfway round the world.

Oil, then as now, was an essential product, and a political minefield.

In November 1951 more British troops flooded into Suez as the Egyptian government declared a state of emergency, and they were still there in July 1954 when it was announced that they would finally leave the Zone by 1956 – which they did. But any thought that the Suez problem was over was short lived. Almost immediately, the president of the new Arab Republic of Egypt, Nasser, seized control of the Canal, and soon after he nationalised its operation, then cut the oil pipelines to the west, making the Canal itself the only direct supply route. An alliance of British and French troops was formed to pressure Nasser into accepting international control of the Canal, but on 31 October after a negotiated solution had clearly failed and Egypt had refused an ultimatum to withdraw, they invaded the disputed area – a move which wasn't universally welcomed either in Britain or by the USA, and which led within nine days to a ceasefire being imposed by the United Nations.

So, as the stand-off continued into 1957, Britain's (and much of Europe's) only oil and fuel supplies were coming the long way round, via the Cape of Good Hope, and petrol was rationed again. At much the same time, the inflation caused by the increased spending of the past few years had put pressure on the pound, and in 1956 the British government had started a 'credit squeeze' - to try to control spending and to make buying luxury goods in particular more difficult.

And luxury goods, of course, included the motor car. So between fuel shortages and credit controls, the new small car stage was set.

BELOW The Suez Crisis led to petrol rationing in the UK during the late 1950s. The country was crying out for a new small car

Chapter 2

The Alternatives

THERE WAS NO DENYING THAT, before the Mini appeared, unusual postwar circumstances had already created some very strange solutions - or rather attempts at solutions. The economic situation around Europe, not only in Britain, was becoming so difficult through the mid 1950s that a new breed of even smaller small car had appeared, and while there were one or two honourable attempts at designing something genuinely innovative, the vast majority of them were crude and in almost every respect awful. Echoing the shape of some of the worst, they were generally called 'bubble cars', and the Suez crisis gave them new life.

Far removed from 'real' small (or affordable) cars like the British Austin and Morris and the basic but conventionally designed Continental equivalents like the Citroen 2CV, the Renault 4, the VW Beetle and the Fiat 500, the bubble cars were motoring reduced to the absolute minimum. The classic goldfish-bowl bubbles were designs like the Italian Isetta and the German Heinkel, typically powered (if that's the word) by air-cooled motorcycle-type engines of less than 250cc and rarely more than a single cylinder. A rare exception was the later 425cc four-

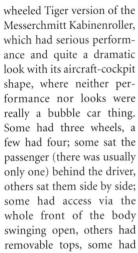

wheeled Tiger version of the Messerchmitt Kabinenroller, which had serious performance and quite a dramatic look with its aircraft-cockpit shape, where neither performance nor looks were really a bubble car thing. Some had three wheels, a few had four; some sat the passenger (there was usually only one) behind the driver, others sat them side by side; some had access via the whole front of the body swinging open, others had removable tops, some had no tops at all so you just stepped over the side into the seats.

But there were bubble cars from all over Europe - from Italy and Germany, from France and Spain, and even from Britain. The BMW-motorcycle-engined Isetta was built under licence in England, as was a version of its lookalike rival the Heinkel, the latter by Trojan of Croydon. There were the three-wheeled, glassfibre-bodied, motorcycle-engined Bonds and Berkeleys (some of which still had the motorcycle kick-start). And then there was the Frisky, a slightly big-

ger but no cleverer 'car' originally designed (ironically given the Suez connection) by a British engineer, Raymond Flower, for the Cairo Motor Company. When the Suez fall-out happened he brought the project back to England where it was built in Wolverhampton – a four-wheeler (with the rear wheels set almost together) powered by a 249cc Villiers two-stroke motorcycle engine. Its two-seater body was almost sporty, its performance wasn't.

And these were the sort of cars that badly irritated one of the big wheels of the British motor industry, Sir Leonard Lord, who in the mid 1950s was chairman of BMC, the British Motor Corporation.

OPPOSITE Bubble cars, such as the Italian Isetta, were a novel but far from practical alternative to conventional small cars in the 1950s

BELOW The British three-wheeled Bond featured a glassfibre body and a motorcycle engine. BMC boss, Leonard Lord, wasn't impressed

Chapter 3

The Man behind the Mini

SIR LEONARD LORD (formerly boss of Morris before Morris and Austin were merged under the BMC umbrella in 1951) led BMC into the decision to build a new small car, in answer to the fuel crisis brought on by Suez. That was in March 1957, and when he said he wanted a small car, he was absolutely adamant about what he didn't want – what he apparently hated with a vengeance. You may have guessed what

that was. 'God damn these bloody awful bubble cars', he was once reported as saying. 'We must drive them off the streets by designing a proper miniature car. . .' By that he meant a car smaller than either of the Corporation's existing small cars, the Morris Minor or the Austin A30, but with maximum passenger space in minimum vehicle size. It had to be proper passenger space, too, for up to four full-sized adults. And the car had to be affordable, but it had to be a real car.

That, in effect, was the brief that Lord gave to the man who would have to turn the idea into reality, his Chief Engineer at BMC, Alec Issigonis.

Without Issigonis, the Mini simply wouldn't have happened, certainly not when it did, probably not ever. And not as such a dramatic and total re-writing of the small-car rulebook. Because the Mini wasn't going to be a car designed by committee, it was Issigonis's vision pure and simple – and Issigonis in 1957 was thinking way outside the box.

He was already a well respected and very clever character indeed, and to understand the Mini you need to understand something about the man – Alexander Arnold Constantine Issigonis. He was born in November 1906 in what was then known as Smyrna (later Izmir) and at the time of Alec's birth that was a part of Turkey (although at other times it was politically a part of Greece). His father, Constantine, was Greek by birth

but having spent a lot of his young, student life in England he had eventually become a naturalized Briton before going back to Smyrna in his mid-thirties. The family business in Smyrna (started by his father, Alec's grandfather) was marine engineering; and Alec's mother Hulda (who Constantine had married at the relatively late age of 35) was the daughter of a wealthy Bavarian who had built the brewery in Smyrna.

All of which should have given young Alec Issigonis a very comfortable childhood, and to a degree it did, but thanks to the political situation while he was growing up it was quite a complicated one, too. Through World War I, as Alec was approaching his teens, Turkey had sided with Germany – so a German-born mother was fine, but a British-naturalized father who refused to let his factory work for the Germans was less good. In fact the family property was confiscated and the family themselves were kept under house arrest until the end of the war. Then, not long after it, with the Greek/Turkish in-fighting leaving Smyrna in ruins, the Issigonis family was evacuated by the British – first to Malta in 1922, then, in 1923, to London. The latter move, sadly, did not include

OPPOSITE Alec Issigonis, the creator of the Mini, in 1958

with a diploma rather than the degree he'd hoped for, because he wasn't good at maths. In 1928, after taking what amounted to a short 'gap-year' with his mother, motoring around Europe, he started his first project in the motor industry, working on the design of an automatic transmission. By the early 1930s he had joined car-maker Humber as a draughtsman, to work on independent suspension designs while those were still rare in the British car industry. And in 1936 he joined Morris, where his boss was Leonard Lord.

When Morris merged with Austin into BMC and looked set to follow a design philosophy that threatened to be far more conservative than the free-thinking Issigonis could handle, he left, and went to Alvis – a British sporting car maker for who he designed a big, fast, expensive luxury car that had an extraordinary list of advanced technical features but which was doomed never to be built, probably because Alvis couldn't afford it.

So in 1956 he went back to BMC, tempted back by his old boss Sir Leonard Lord to join the Austin Design Office at Longbridge near Oxford, and to become the company's Chief

Alec's seriously ill father, who had had to be left behind in Malta, where he died before his wife could get back to him. So Alec and his mother now began a completely new life in England – and in fact never lived apart for almost the next fifty years, until Hulda died in 1972, when Alec was in his mid sixties and had just retired from his life in the motor industry.

Back in the mid 1920s, he had started to train as an engineer, at Battersea Polytechnic, from where he emerged

Engineer. Which was exactly where he was and what he was doing as the Suez crisis unfolded, and when Lord came to him with the brief to build his new small car.

First time around with Morris he had already designed one car that would have qualified as most designers' masterpiece, the Morris Minor. He had started thinking about it even before the war ended, when he was also working on projects for military use, including a lightweight reconnaissance vehicle and a small amphibian with an outboard motor, both for the army. While he was doing that he was also designing independent suspensions for MG, and in the early 1940s he started a project called Mosquito that would become his first complete car design and one of the best known of all British cars, the Morris Minor.

When it was launched, in 1948, it wasn't quite as innovative as Issigonis had wanted it to be, with a two-stroke flat-four engine, but it did have a unique combination of other advanced features (like unit

body construction where most still had a separate chassis, and torsion bar suspension where most had coil or cart springs). As such, after the postwar design stagnation, it was widely acclaimed as Britain's first 'modern' small car. It would also have a very long and profitable production life, and it would establish Issigonis as a designer to watch. But his next project would make him famous forever.

BELOW The Morris Minor, which was launched in 1948, was Issigonis's first masterpiece and was very modern and innovative in its day

Chapter 4

The Solution

BEYOND THE 'REAL CAR, SMALL CAR' brief, Sir Leonard Lord had imposed only two other demands on Issigonis: that he should use an engine already available from the BMC range, and that the car should be production-ready within two years – which was an exceptionally tough call.

It started as project ADO 15, ADO for the Austin Drawing Office. As he had with the Minor, Issigonis started sketching ideas, eventually passing the detail on to more skilled draftsmen. He accepted early on that he would use BMC's compact (and low cost) A-Series engine, from the Minor, the A30 and several others. And he set himself a target of an overall package ten feet long by four feet wide

by four feet tall. That was enough to accommodate Lord's four full-size passengers but was clearly not achievable with a conventional front-engine, rear-drive layout and booted saloon shape. It could be possible, though, if he turned the engine sideways, drove the front wheels, and settled for a 'bootless' two-box layout rather than the usual three-box saloon shape.

It wasn't that simple, obviously. Crucially, he had to accommodate the

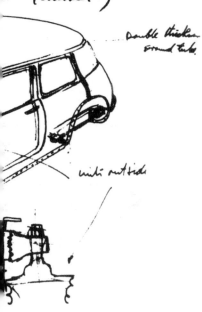

Petrol tank (stressed.)

Double thickness around tube.

unit outside

developed by Dunlop), plus drum brakes compact enough to fit inside. He also needed an unusually compact suspension layout and driveshaft joints to accommodate steering as well as suspension movement. The first problem was solved by another touch of genius, using a rubber and metal cone spring system developed by Issigonis's long-time friend Alex Moulton. The rubber springs took up minimal space, and also worked whether the car was fully laden or with just a driver; and they allowed smaller, lighter dampers because they had some built-in damping effect of their own. For the driveshafts he used special metal outer joints with simple flexible inner couplings.

He kept costs down by using simple external body seams rather than more expensive flush welding, and used external door hinges – both features which, almost by chance, gave the Mini strong styling features, even though it had never been styled at all in the accepted sense. In fact Issigonis scorned the idea of style in the sense of fashion – designing almost solely for function. He

gearbox. Leaving it on the end of the engine would make it too long to fit under the bonnet; putting it behind (as in alongside) the engine would either eat into passenger space or make the car too long. So in a stroke of genius he put it in effect underneath the engine, but incorporated it into a specially designed oil sump, with only the final drive behind it.

The other revolutionary move was the tiny, ten-inch-diameter wheels – which needed special tyres (initially

MIDDLE An early Issigonis sketch for the Mini clearly shows the clever packaging. Note the petrol tank under the bonnet!

ABOVE Alex Moulton, who designed the original Mini's novel suspension, in 1963 on another of his creations - the rubber sprung Moulton bicycle

reduced other normally complicated solutions to basics, cutting costs without ever cutting functionality. Simple string door pulls and sliding windows were cheap to make and freed the doors of linkages and winding mechanisms – leaving valuable storage space without sacrificing passenger space. Admittedly there wasn't much conventional boot space (he said he didn't believe in it) but he created remarkable amounts of oddment stowage inside, in the doors, in the rear body sides, on the simple dashboard shelf and even under the rear seats. And if you did have more cases than the boot would take, you could

drop the lid on its strong retaining cords and use it as an additional carrier. In its details the design was clever, in its entirety it was brilliant.

Amazingly, too, Issigonis was delivering the project on time, in spite of that almost impossible schedule. Within four months of getting the go-ahead he and his tiny team had built the first mock-ups, and three months after that most of his sketches had been formalised as engineering drawings and two prototypes (disguised as A30s) had been built – painted orange and inevitably nicknamed Orange Boxes.

The biggest change from prototype

towards production was to turn the engine round so the exhaust and carburettor were behind the block rather than in front – but although that kept the carb out of the elements as intended, it gave a new set of problems in waterproofing the ignition, and it meant an extra set of gears to change the direction of the drive around – which added weight and sapped a bit of power. They improved the gearshift, brakes and engine and suspension mountings, but in one respect they took an apparently backward step, swapping the 37bhp 948cc engine for a 34bhp 848cc one – because they thought the 90mph+ top speed of the prototypes was more than the customer would be comfortable with, so the new maximum was about 72mph.

Those changes took the project into 1958, and in the summer Sir Leonard Lord drove one of the revised cars briefly and almost immediately signed the project off for production, with a 'Job One' target of one year.

The next prototypes were very close to launch specification, the final half dozen were in effect pre-production cars, and finally a handful of cars were hand-built on each of the two production lines (at Longbridge for Austins and Cowley for Morrises), to prove that they worked, too.

By June 1959 they were building cars in substantial numbers ready for the launch. And in the end they launched it a few days before they had originally planned, on that famous day, 26 August 1959. Mini Day.

BELOW The first prototypes had the engine the other way round, with the carburettor at the front. A30 grille was a disguise

Chapter 5

Onto the Road

BY THE VERY NATURE of its convention-defying looks and layout, the original Mini was guaranteed to grab headlines, and it did. On the very day that it first appeared in dealer's showrooms, the first driving impressions and technical appreciations also appeared in the press – the first journalists having been invited to drive the car just over a week before its public unveiling. And even the most demanding and hard-bitten of testers knew that this was a car a long way out of the ordinary. As the authoritative weekly The Motor said in its first ever review of the Mini,

'Characteristics which have often been thought utterly incompatible are combined amazingly well in the new 848cc Austin Seven. . .'

Badges and grilles aside, the Morris version was to all intents and purposes identical to the Austin one, and called the Mini-Minor. Both names echoed small cars from different eras in the past for what in 1959 was called BMC, the British Motor Company, creators of the Mini. The original Austin 7 was one of the most significant small cars in British motoring history, built from 1922 to 1939, while Austin and Morris were still independent entities, and long before they had merged under the BMC umbrella in 1951. It was a small car for a big market, at a time when motoring for the masses was a relatively new notion. And the Mini-Minor name obviously referred to Issigonis's earlier masterpiece, the Minor. Which suggests that they planned a big future for their new small car.

And it was still a small car, because all Issigonis's revolutionary thinking had survived from concept to reality, and the car as it hit the showrooms was recognisably the same animal as the Man from Izmir had sketched on tablecloths and cigarette packets at the outset of the project. Which in a nutshell meant a car that genuinely was only ten feet long but which could accommodate four adults in reasonable comfort and swallow a

surprising amount of luggage and oddments. It sat on those mould-breaking ten-inch wheels, wrapped around their specially developed drum brakes, and it sat on the innovative rubber-sprung suspension developed by Issigonis's friend Alex Moulton. It had its 848cc, 34bhp version of the A-Series engine, set transversely across the front of the car, now with the carburettors and exhaust system at the 'back', between the engine and the front bulkhead, and the distributor rather worryingly exposed to the elements at the 'front', just behind the grille.

The gearbox, of course, was under the crankshaft, in what was normally just

OPPOSITE 1959 Austin Seven on the road

ABOVE Prime Minister Harold Macmillan admires the new Morris Mini Minor at the 1959 Earls Court Motor Show

ABOVE An early promotional photograph showing an Austin Seven with all the luggage it could supposedly carry!

the oil sump, but which in the Mini's case doubled up as a very substantial gearbox casing. And the final drive unit was behind the engine, driving the front wheels through those relatively simple driveshafts with their rubber inner joints and Rzeppa outer ones. It really was a fantastic piece of packaging, and its looks took care of themselves.

The press reports after the preview drives should have given the new car a flying start when it came to convincing the market that it worked. One magazine, The Autocar, took their test car on a marathon 8200-mile trip around

Europe which generated four weeks of magazine stories. They averaged almost exactly 36mpg, covered as much as 662 miles in one 24-hour marathon stint, and aside from overheating problems, problems with that rather exposed ignition distributor in wet weather, and broken damper mountings, almost nothing went wrong.

That was all the more remarkable given the pace of development, so the snag-fixing continued even as the production gathered pace – helped by a team of unofficial test drivers, as the company had lent a large number of brand new Minis to members of the motoring press for extended, six-month test drives. And they all seemed to love them.

And it's worth remembering just what a revolution the Mini was in the small car ranks in 1959. Forget about the bubble cars now – they were effectively dead and buried once the Mini was launched. But while the rest of the small car opposition wasn't about to curl up and die just because the Mini had arrived, cars like the Mini's BMC cousin the Austin A30 certainly started to look ordinary with their conventional rear-drive layouts and three-box saloon shapes. When you look at other Mini rivals, too, like the square-backed Pininfarina-styled Austin A40 and Ford's new Anglia (launched at much the same time as the Mini) with its backward sloping rear window, it's hard to believe they were contemporaries. Nearly fifty years on, a classic Mini hardly looks out of place on the road, where any one of those 1959 rivals simply looks ancient.

Every one of them, too, was considerably bigger than the Mini externally, yet few offered significantly more usable space internally. Only the 105E Anglia with its excellent new overhead valve engine and slick four-speed gearbox was quicker than the Mini, by a few mph, but it was also quite a bit more expensive – as was any other alternative.

Remarkably, though, none of what we now think of as the Mini's strengths immediately convinced the notoriously conservative British car-buying public of the late 1950s that they had to have this amazing newcomer. And while it undoubtedly had its teething problems

as already hinted at, the bigger problems in the early days of the Mini's sales life was actually a lot more to do with image than with reality.

To put it politely, the typical British family car buyer in the late 1950s (and for all its minimal size, the Mini was a family car) was a lot more interested in making the right social impression than in driving the cleverest engineering solution. So the Mini now faced a crisis point. . .

ABOVE The interior of the first Mini was spartan but roomy, with a handy shelf for your handbag, sunglasses and Camel cigarettes!

Chapter 6

Acceptance

THE MINI MAY HAVE BEEN incredibly clever, good to drive and deceptively practical, but when it first appeared it had one major problem that had nothing to do with its engineering. At the time of its launch, the Mini design was proving to be a lot more open-minded than the people it was designed for, and to put it at its simplest, it wasn't selling at all well.

The problem wasn't that the Mini was particularly expensive. It wasn't the cheapest small car on the market, but it wasn't far off. Of the 'real' cars you could buy in Britain in 1959, only the old and very basic Ford Popular was significantly cheaper, at £419 – when the cheapest Mini (which had very few frills indeed) was offered at £497, and the Austin Seven 850 Super De Luxe (with luxuries like a heater!) cost just over £537, of which not quite £159, or almost 30 per cent of the total, was tax. And when Ford's new rival, the Anglia, was launched at virtually the same time as the Mini, in 1959, it cost a hefty £589 – almost precisely the same as a Morris Minor, which was BMC's conventional alternative to the Mini.

The Mini did have mechanical teething problems, too, as we've already seen, but it would have been even more surprising if it hadn't had the odd glitch, given the ground-breaking nature of the design and the spectacular speed with which it had been brought to production. And one of the early faults in particular clearly showed how the pace of the development occasionally meant the engineers hadn't seen the wood for the trees. In short, when it was wet, the Mini leaked, letting in water through the floor and soaking first the carpets then the feet. There was a joke at the time that you got a pair of Wellingtons with every new Mini, but for the people trying to have the car taken seriously, it wasn't funny.

They spent a lot of time and money trying to work out where the water was coming in, driving through water splashes with engineers laying on the floor trying to see what was happening, and failing. They tried filling the door sills with foam, but that didn't do it; and nor did any other 'cure' until somebody realised that where the two-piece floor on the early cars was joined, across the car, the joint was overlapped the opposite way around to how it had been on the prototypes (which hadn't leaked).

BELOW On 7th October 1965 Peter Sellers drove a Radford De Ville Mini out of a giant birthday cake. It was a present for wife Britt Ekland. The Stunt took place on Radford's 2nd anniversary!

ABOVE Mike Nesmith of the Monkees with what was at the time the most expensive Mini ever, a Radford-built Cooper S

So instead of keeping water out, the joint was scooping it in.

They soon cured that one, and they worked their way through other problems, too. They made the wheels stronger to stop the centres pulling out as more enthusiastic drivers discovered the Mini's amazing cornering power, and they stiffened up the engine mountings to stop the exhaust pipe breaking as the engine moved around. They improved the crankshaft oil seal to keep oil away from the clutch, they introduced quieter, multi-bladed cooling fans because the original four-bladed one made a high-pitched screaming noise at high speeds, and they made major improvements to the quality of the gearchange, by introducing a new kind of 'baulk-ring' syncromesh in 1962 – by which time the Mini was a far better car than the version that had first been rushed into production.

Yet none of this was the main reason why the Mini wasn't exactly a runaway success in its early days. In the four months remaining of 1959 after its August launch, 19,749 cars came off the production lines. And in its first full year, 1960, they sold just 116,677 cars, which wasn't nearly enough if the Mini was going to survive in a very tough market.

What was really holding the Mini back in those early days was a far more worrying problem – one that couldn't be solved just by nuts and bolts. The people who were supposed to be buying the Mini just didn't want to stand out in the way the Mini did, as low-priced and unusual. They weren't even impressed by its low running costs and excellent economy. Cars, even small, low cost cars, were still status symbols, and in a society where bigger was generally better, the Mini didn't have buyer appeal.

And, however good it really was, that alone might have been enough to kill the Mini in its infancy had the story not taken a strange twist. Because what happened was that while the working classes who the car was aimed at were turning their back on it, the 'smart set' from the classes above suddenly adopted it as a style statement – a car they could fit into the traffic in Chelsea or Kensington and which, perversely, they saw as a lot more stylish than any of its small-car rivals!

It was adopted by film stars and models, the rock-set and the design world. In no time at all, it seemed, you could find Peter Sellers in a whole series of ever more exotic Minis, and his fellow Goon Spike Milligan even appeared in an advertisement for BMC because he thought the Mini was a truly patriotic car.

ABOVE Lord Snowdon and Princess Margaret were young and popular in the 1960s. When they bought a Mini, people took notice!

The Beatles had Minis, and so did Lulu. A few years later, in the mid-1960s, Monkee Mike Nesmith had what was then the most expensive Mini of all specially built for himself, by Mini coachbuilding specialists Radford. It had a tuned 1275cc Cooper S engine and a very luxurious interior, with air-conditioning, a very exotic radio and tape-player system, and a price tag of £3640 (without tax, because he was taking it abroad), or seven times the cost of the first Mini.

Actors like Laurence Harvey, Hayley Mills and Jenny Agutter all took to the Mini, as did models like Jean Shrimpton and Twiggy. Even all-American legend (and enthusiastic racing driver) Steve McQueen was a Mini fan. And although the Minis of the stars were almost always very, very different and far more exotic than the basic item, the effect on the lower end of the market was the same – the Mini was suddenly chic.

But most significantly of all, the Mini was adopted by the upper classes beyond the movies and rock-and-roll – even by royalty. Princess Grace of Monaco started to drive one around the Principality. And most famously of all, after Alec Issigonis had driven the Queen around Hyde Park in a Mini, her sister and brother-in-law, Princess Margaret and society photographer Lord Snowdon, became Mini fans too – and Snowdon even became a good friend of Issigonis, which Issigonis loved.

At a stroke, the Mini – without really changing at all - wasn't a small, strange, cheap, un-stylish motorised shoebox for the working classes any more, it was a classy, classless status symbol. And all of a sudden, they could hardly build them fast enough. From that life-threatening trickle of fewer than 120,000 cars in 1960, annual sales turned into a torrent. In 1961 they passed 150,000, in 1965 the

millionth Mini rolled off the line, and by the end of the 'sixties they had passed the two million total and were selling more than a quarter of a million a year.

The Mini was now clearly here to stay, and to evolve. . .

BELOW If Steve McQueen drove a Mini, they had to be cool cars!

Chapter 7

Minis with More

ALREADY BY THE MID 1960S, THE Mini was becoming a phenomenon way beyond the usual car mould. Those up-market Mini enthusiasts had almost all, to some extent or other, turned their Minis into pint-sized luxury cars, loaded with wood and leather, special creature-comfort equipment, and more often than not an extra level of performance too. Very few 'ordinary' Mini buyers left their car standard for long, either, and beyond all the off-the-shelf higher specification models like the earliest De Luxe, and beyond all the little extras you could buy from BMC themselves, a whole industry began to spring up, offering more for the Mini, from performance, to comfort, to luggage space, to looks.

At the top end of the new specialist Mini tweakers there were the money-no-object coachbuilders and tuners who catered for the film star and royalty end of the market – names like Wood & Pickett, Harold Radford (Coachbuilders), Hoopers, and the brilliant tuning wizards Downton could all transform the Mini into diminutive Rolls-Royce clones. At a price, as cars like Mike Nesmith's and Peter Sellers' famously proved. But for those on a more modest budget, there were more modest Mini modifiers, too.

They could sell you goodies off the shelf to turn your Mini into almost anything you wanted it to be, from the sublime to the ridiculous. You could get really simple bolt-on extras that made it nicer to drive – like gearlever extensions, better-shaped throttle pedals and more adjustment for your driving seat, even completely different seats; they could sell you bits to make your Mini stand out from the herd – from little chrome eyebrows to go over the headlamps to fake wicker side panels, just like the ones Peter Sellers used to love; they could sell you roof racks and ugly tack-on boots to carry more luggage, and larger, long-range fuel tanks to take you further

between garage visits; they could sell you things to improve refinement and reliability – tie-bars to stop the engine rocking and stronger links to stop the exhaust pipe breaking.

But probably most prominently of all, they could sell you sporty performance that the original Mini never dreamed of, but which was now becoming just as much of a defining point of the Mini as its size.

It wasn't that Mini-creator Alec Issigonis didn't have any interest in per-

ABOVE This Radford Mini from 1971 features unique headlamps, wheelarch extensions and a full-length sunroof

OPPOSITE Built in 1968 for Prince Temenggeng Mohamed Belkiah of Brunei by John Sprinzel and Wood & Pickett, this unique Mini Cooper S cost over £4000

formance – he did, and he even had experience in motor sport, as a car designer, constructor and driver. But in the beginning he had never thought of the Mini as anything other than a utility car, certainly not the performance icon and multiple race and rally winner that it would become. As he said himself, 'when the Mini was designed and went into production, I never gave competition motoring a single thought. We were preoccupied in the design with getting good roadholding and stability, but for safety reasons, and to give the driver more pleasure. It never occurred to me that this thing would turn out to be such a successful rally car'. There's no doubt at all, though, that when the Mini did start racing, he loved it.

His direct motor sport links, admittedly, were some time in the past, but they actually did have some influence on the Mini story. And appropriately, they started way back in the 1930s with the Mini's spiritual ancestor, the original Austin Seven. Issigonis started like many other drivers did at the time, by building increasingly sporty versions of the Seven, but then, with an engineer friend George Dowson, he created a car of his own design, a compact, streamlined, front-engined single-seater that he could drive in hillclimbs, sprints and circuit racers. He called it the Lightweight Special, and he used his contacts in the Austin works racing department to acquire a very special supercharged 60bhp 750cc side-valve Austin Seven racing engine and the gearbox to go with it. But the car he put it in was entirely his own design and construction, and for its day it incorporated some extremely advanced design features.

He created it much as he would create the Mini a quarter of a century later – with sketches rather than formal engineering drawings, which he and George Dowson then turned into their race car. And like the Mini, it didn't owe much to conventional thinking, not for the 1930s.

The 'Lightweight' part of its name was the first key to its success. It didn't have a chassis in the traditional 1930s sense of a ladder frame or anything like; instead, it had deep body sides made from plywood sheathed in aluminium sheet and sandwiching front and rear bulkheads, the seat, and the engine, gearbox and rear axle mountings. It was far stiffer than a ladder-framed car, and a lot lighter, at only about 1100lb complete. Unusually for even a racing car in its day, it had all independent suspension; and even more unusually the suspension (which could be significantly softer than the norm because of the car's

BELOW Crayford began building convertible Minis in the early 1960s

ABOVE Issisgonis built this Lightweight Special using an Austin Seven as the basis

They finished building it in 1938 and both Issigonis and Dowson drove it – showing its potential by beating the similarly-powered works Austin racers at Prescott hillclimb, but being sidelined by the war before they could develop it further. Suggesting how advanced the design was, though, it started winning again in the late 1940s when the war was over, and with an overhead camshaft engine developed by Issigonis and Dowson in 1947 it carried on racing until Issigonis's new bosses at BMC told him he wasn't allowed to race anymore because he was too valuable to them.

But in 1946 at the Brighton Speed Trials, the Lightweight Special had an even more important effect on the future Mini story, in bringing Issigonis into contact with another innovative young racing car designer, one John Cooper. On the Madeira Drive sprint course, Issigonis's Lightweight Special took on Cooper's first 500cc Cooper Special – the forerunner of a whole generation of motorcycle-engined single-seater Formula 3 cars from the pioneer of the mid-engined racing car. And while Cooper beat Issigonis that day, they became very good friends.

Fast forward again now to the early

unusually light weight) used rubber rather than steel springs as the suspension medium – just as the Mini would (in a different way) more than twenty years later.

Just as in the Mini, rubber springs saved weight and complexity and gave a certain amount of natural damping as well as progressive-rate springing, and that gave the Lightweight Special exceptionally good roadholding to go with its better than usual power-to-weight ratio.

days of the Mini in production, and the discovery that it was potentially a lot more than just a city car. Because if neither Issigonis himself nor the people who tested the prototype had made a big thing of it, a lot of owners were starting to notice it – the Mini had astonishingly good roadholding. Good enough, in fact, to let the Mini way outperform its modest power. So within

weeks of its launch, the first enthusiasts were taking near-enough standard Minis to events like sprints and driving tests, and proving that on the right kind of track, with its compactness and agility, it could run rings round far more powerful opposition, just as the Lightweight Special had.

When it first took to the tracks with not much more than its standard

BELOW Right from the start, people took near-standard Minis onto the racetrack. This car is leading a Ford Anglia and another Mini at Silverstone in 1961

ABOVE Minis were lots of fun to race, as this 1961 shot taken at Goodwood demonstrates

screaming, darting through gaps that shouldn't have existed, and generally rewriting the rule books for saloon car racing.

It had scored its first class win before the end of 1959, driven by 'Doc' Shepherd at Snetterton. And by 1961 it had won its first big title, the British Saloon Car Championship, where Sir John Whitmore didn't only win his class but won the series outright, too, against much bigger opposition.

It lost occasionally because the racing Minis exaggerated the problems of the production cars and things broke (like wheels and exhausts and clutches). In fact the wheel problem was so bad at an early Six-Hour Relay race at Silverstone that all Minis with the original steel wheels were actually banned from racing in Britain – but just as with the road cars they gradually solved the problems, and every Mini benefited.

The phenomenon did not go unnoticed by the people who made the Mini, either, and that was where Issigonis's old rivalry, turned into a long friendship, with John Cooper opened another chapter in the Mini story.

34bhp, it obviously wasn't very fast in a straight line, but in the corners it gave the bigger cars a very hard time indeed, and would carry on doing so for a good many years to come, on road and track. Anyone who laughed at the Mini when it turned up to race for the first time soon stopped laughing when they saw what a giant-killer it could be. And it didn't just beat its small rear-drive rivals, it could frighten real sports cars, and even much bigger saloons. It was also a fantastic sight to watch, powering through the bends with smoke billowing from the front tyres and the rubber

Enter the Cooper

IN THE YEARS SINCE HE HAD raced against Issigonis, while Alec had in effect been banned from competing by his employers, John Cooper had moved into higher echelons of motor racing, through his original 500cc Formula 3 cars, sports cars, and eventually into the pinnacle of the sport, in Grand Prix racing. He was credited with pioneering the modern mid-engined chassis layout, with the engine behind the driver but ahead of the rear wheels, just as every serious single-seater racing car has been since.

By the time the Mini was taking its first steps in competition, Cooper had already won the Formula 1 world championship as a constructor, and built a very successful business selling off-the-shelf racing cars to a grow-

ing market for formulae based on production engines that Cooper himself had pioneered and helped to grow. He built the cars that helped future legends

ABOVE The first Mini Coopers didn't look that different to the standard car

make their first steps in the racing world – from Stirling Moss to Jack Brabham, Bruce McLaren to Graham Hill.

And he kept in touch with Alec Issigonis – so when the Mini appeared with one of the engines that Cooper knew best of all, the four-cylinder A-Series, Cooper started to see some intriguing possibilities.

Like the movie stars, models, rock heroes and royalty, top level racing driv-

ers had also taken to the Mini as a road car – in their case not so much because of its handiness in town or its classless chic, but because of that astonishing, giant-killing handling. And when even his Formula 1 drivers like Brabham and McLaren started to drive Minis, Cooper gave them a bit more power – from the A-Series engine he knew so well.

Then in 1961, the inevitable happened, and Cooper suggested to Issigonis

that a roadgoing Mini with more power and performance might not be a bad idea now that the car seemed to have found its identity. All of which was of considerable interest to BMC's bosses, too – who had decided that competition really could play a part in the Mini's future, and who needed a production car to base such a future on, built and sold in sufficient numbers to satisfy the rules for production-based racers.

So John Cooper was officially commissioned to produce just such a car, and like Issigonis with the original Mini, he delivered it in record time. He gave it more power with a bigger version

of the A-Series engine, up from 848cc to 997cc, plus a modified cylinder head and exhaust system, and twin SU carburettors to get more fuel mixture in and out. He improved the gearshift with a remote linkage instead of the original long lever, and gave the car the power to stop as well as to go by adding front disc brakes – at the time, the smallest disc brakes on any production car.

As with the original Mini, the BMC bosses drove it, loved it, and agreed to pay Cooper a £2 royalty on every car they made with his name on it – as the Mini Cooper. They may not have thought they could sell the 1000 cars

ABOVE Mini Coopers were an instant hit on the track as well as the road

ABOVE LEFT John Cooper in the early 1960s. A man whose name will be forever linked to the Mini

997cc engine gave an extra 21bhp, up from 34 to 55, or a remarkable 62 per cent increase over the basic car! That improved top speed by 15mph to 88mph, and carved the 0-60mph acceleration time down from around 30 seconds (which believe it or not was considered quite sparkling for a small family car in 1959) to an impressive 18 seconds. The closer-ratio gearbox with its much shorter shift, the stronger brakes and retuned suspension all helped make the Cooper a very different car from the standard Mini, too, and it was an instant hit, on road and track.

It was the Mini Coopers, of course, that began to rack up the competition successes; and it was the competition successes that proved the old adage – win races on Sunday, sell cars on Monday. And for Mini and Cooper, the successes came thick and fast over the next decade and beyond, in every conceivable kind of motor sport, and around the world.

demanded by the racing rules, but in September 1961, only months after Cooper's first suggestion, the Mini Cooper went on sale. And it's fair to say that the coming of the Mini Cooper did almost as much to consolidate the image of the Mini in those troubled early days as the film stars and royals had done in their own way. Now Mini meant sporty, too.

In fact the first Mini Cooper was already a pretty impressive package. Its

In 1962 BMC ran an ad headed 'Competition Scoopers, these Mini Coopers', listing the cars' international successes that year. Which included the British Saloon Car Championship again (this time for John Love), class wins at Snetterton, Goodwood, Aintree, Silverstone, Crystal Palace, Mallory Park, Oulton Park and Brands Hatch, and further afield in the Coupe des Bruxelles, the Prix Vienne, the 12-Hour Sedan Race in Washington, the saloon race at the German Grand Prix at the Nurburgring, and even an outright win at Chartres. And Mini Coopers also took first, second and third places in the 1-litre class in the Swedish championship.

A year later, Dutchman Rob Sloetemaker added the European 1300cc title with the new Cooper S (of which more anon), then in 1964 Mini won an astonishing haul, with Warren Banks taking both the British and European 1-litre class wins, plus the European title outright, while John Fitpatrick also won the 1300cc class in another Cooper S!

Even that, though, was barely the start. That first Cooper S had been launched as a road car in March 1963 and it was one of the greatest Minis of all. To spread the Cooper's wings first into the 1100cc racing ranks, it had a capacity of 1071cc, and many special internal parts like pistons, valves and camshafts that were all just starting points for the equally important racing engines. In 1071 form, with big bores and short strokes, they were smooth, high-revving screamers with lots of power. Even for the road, the first Cooper S offered 70bhp (another huge leap), almost 95mph, and 0-60mph in

BELOW By today's standards this 1967 Cooper S looks fairly tame, its only distinguishing mark being the 'John Cooper S' badge on the bonnet

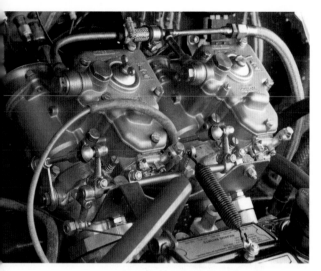

ABOVE This 1968 Cooper S engine is equipped with twin Weber carburettors

dreamed possible, creating their own halo effect.

Next up, in January 1964, the short-stroke 998cc Cooper replaced the long-stroke 997, with an engine that was no more powerful but was more flexible, more reliable and easier to tune for competition. The one downside, also in 1964, was that like the mainstream Minis the Coopers switched from the brilliant original rubber suspension to the gas-filled Hydrolastic system, which claimed to make the Mini more comfortable but never matched the 'dry' cars for grip or handling. And unfortunately that survived until 1971, which was exactly the same lifespan as the first generation Mini Coopers; but that's getting ahead of the story.

For a while in 1964, again with an eye on the racing classes, there were three different Cooper Ss, with 970, 1071 and 1275cc versions, for 1-litre, 1100 and 1300cc British and European racing campaigns – with the results that season that we've just mentioned above. All three engines were based on the same cylinder block, the faithful A-Series, which meant that BMC were getting a lot for their money from the Cooper programme. The 1275 was first to

less than 13 seconds. Which for 1963 was very quick indeed, and further enhanced by an even stronger gearbox, wider wheels, and more powerful servo-assisted brakes. Combined with the Mini's already legendary handling, it was a sensational package.

The Mini Cooper family kept growing, too, driven jointly by the chance to take on new racing classes and an astonishing demand for Cooper-badged road cars – which were selling in far greater numbers than the management ever

appear after the original 1071, in April 1964, with the longest possible stroke, the most power and the most torque of any of the roadgoing S engines. In this case that meant 76bhp and 79lb ft of torque, which was almost twice as much as the original Mini's 44lb ft. That took it very close to 100mph, with 0-60mph in less than eleven seconds, which was starting to look seriously fast for such a small car, and was.

That wasn't only the biggest engined Cooper S, it was the biggest seller too, by some margin. And at the other end of the scale was the 970cc S with its very short stroke and high revving character. That made it a fantastic 1-litre racer but a bit frantic as a road car – so fewer than 1000 were sold, actually a few short of what the racing rules required. It was another stunning performer though, close to the 1275 on top speed and the 1071 on acceleration, but not easy to live with on the road.

That wasn't the point, though; primarily the baby S, even more than the others, was about racing – and all the Coopers continued to deliver. On the racetrack the main attack generally came from the Mini Coopers in the Grand Prix colours of dark green with a white

roof and white bonnet stripes, while on the rally stages the favoured colour was red with white roof and white stripes – both of which naturally became popular colour schemes for the Cooper road cars, too. And while the 'works' rally cars were always run directly by the Competition Department at Abingdon, near Oxford (which was also the home of MG), the 'works' race cars were always run by outside teams such as Cooper, Broadspeed, and in 1964 and 1965 even by Cooper's Grand Prix rival Tyrrell,

BELOW An early Mini Cooper engine, with its distinctive twin SU's

ABOVE In 1275 form, this Cooper S is competing in the 1968 Monte Carlo Rally

who entered Banks' 1964 European Saloon Car Championship winning car.

The full competition cars grew more and more powerful through this 1960s heyday, too. Even the 1-litre cars could eventually give 120bhp, and the fuel injected 1300 Coopers from 1968 with their crossflow cylinder heads gave as much as 140bhp, which was about as much as the Mini's front wheels could

reasonably handle in those days when the cars were still running on ten-inch wheels and what today we'd think of as relatively narrow tyres. It made for spectacular racing, though, with Mini geniuses like John 'Smokey' Rhodes perfecting the art of the tyre-smoking power-on drift and becoming the most successful of all the works Mini drivers. Against serious rivals like 1968 1-litre

British Saloon Car Champion Gordon Spice, Fitzpatrick, Banks and former rally star John Handley, Rhodes won the 1300 class of the British Saloon Car Championship no fewer than four times in a row between 1965 and 1968 – and in 1969 he scored maybe the Mini's biggest ever giant-killing race win, by winning outright at the Salzburgring in Austria against unlimited capacity opposition. And this, remember, at a time when the Mini had already been around for ten years.

It obviously couldn't last forever, of course, but even when Ford started to take on the Minis with the new Escort, they still put up a fight. In 1968, Handley, driving for the works-backed British Vita Racing team won another European championship outright; and in 1969, when the yellow and black Coopers were officially run by Abingdon, the overall title was stolen by Equipe Arden and driver Alec Poole with a 1-litre Cooper!

And amazingly, even then it wasn't over – not by almost another decade. In 1969, Richard Longman burst onto the Mini racing scene and just kept winning. He was still doing it in 1977 with Patrick Motors sponsorship when he won outright at Donington and Brands Hatch in the new and hugely competitive Group 1 category. Then even more astonishingly, he took both the 1978 and 1979 RAC British Saloon Car Championship titles outright, by dominating the 1300 class. But that, finally, after twenty years at the top, really was the end of the beginning.

BELOW The Cooper and Cooper S dominated motorsport throughout the 1960s, despite being challenged by the new Ford Escort towards the end of the decade

Chapter 9

Do It Yourself!

IF YOU WANTED MINI PERFORMANCE direct from the production line, the Mini Coopers and Cooper Ss were the perfect answer, but they weren't the only answer – or for some people even a workable answer. For all its newfound up-market fan club and its high profile racetrack enterprises, it is worth remembering that the Mini was born as a low-cost car for ordinary people who didn't have the funds to buy anything much more expensive. And quick as the Coopers were, they did cost quite a bit more than the less powerful standard models. At its launch in 1959, the Mini was genuinely one of the cheapest 'real' small cars on the road, at just £497 for the absolute base-specification models.

When the first Mini Cooper was unveiled in September 1961 it cost £679, and the classic, 1275 Cooper S cost an even more substantial £695 when it joined the family in 1964.

So it's hardly surprising that for every Cooper sold, they sold around forty standard Minis. But the fact was that every standard Mini (even every cut-price second-hand Mini as those started to come onto the market) was also a

OPPOSITE Paddy Hopkirk was one of the first big names in Mini tuning

LEFT Janspeed offered a range of tuning parts, in particular sports exhaust systems

more special Mini just waiting to happen. And pretty soon, there was a whole industry that could make it happen.

It was a situation that meant almost no two Minis on the road in the early 1960s and beyond were exactly identical, because almost everyone who drove one wanted to be an individual – not necessarily to the extremes of money-no-object fans like Sellers and Nesmith, but with aspirations to suit their pock-

ets and personal preferences. So you could make your Mini, however humble the starting point, more comfortable, more eye-catching, more user-friendly and, especially, more powerful.

It was a well-established process that Mini brought out of the specialist car shadows and right into the mainstream, with bolt-on performance you could literally buy off the shelf and apply for yourself, rather than having to hand the

ABOVE Uprated dampers offered a sure way of improving the Mini's already great handling

car over to the old-style tuning wizard. And you could add a significant amount of go for very little dough.

It didn't even have to be major surgery, because performance really hadn't been much of a priority on the standard car – in fact you might recall that they actually cut back on engine capacity, power and performance during the development stage when they realised that the Orange Box prototypes were rather quicker than they had intended.

So you could get a significant improvement, for instance, just by changing external parts like the carburettor and the exhaust system – even just changing the carburettor needle and bolting on a bigger-bore 'straight-through' exhaust made the Mini a bit livelier, and just as important for some people, made it sound a lot more sporty. But once you got to the insides of the A-Series engine, the scope was enormous.

The fact was, of course, that that engine had been around for a lot longer than the Mini itself, in everything from the humble Morris Minor to screaming Formula Junior single-seater racing cars, so plenty of people knew exactly how to wring more out of it. And as the old racing adage goes, 'speed costs money, how fast do you want to go?' It was your call.

The next stage, typically, was to improve the cylinder head and the valve gear, to get more fuel mixture in and out of the engine more often, and to burn it more efficiently. You could do all of those by reshaping the combustion chambers, opening out and smoothing the inlet and exhaust ports, putting in bigger valves plus lighter pushrods and rocker gear to let them open and close a bit quicker without bouncing and destroying themselves, and raising the compression ratio - all to give a bigger bang on each power stroke. And you could do all of that without even taking the engine out of the car, just by taking the head off the engine.

Then you could get into more serious territory, inside the cylinder block. You could replace the single camshaft with something more aggressive, that gave the valves more lift and kept them open for longer. You could change the gears and the chain that drove the camshaft from the crankshaft, to make them lighter but more durable, so you could make the engine rev harder, which is the other classic way to more power and performance. You could fit lighter, stronger pistons, and a stronger, better balanced crankshaft. And you could lighten the flywheel to make the engine more responsive. You could uprate the ignition system (a simple coil and distribu-

tor layout originally, long before the era of electronic engine management), and uprate the lubrication system to make sure it all stayed in one piece – including fitting the little oil-cooling radiator that clearly announced to the outside world that this Mini was special.

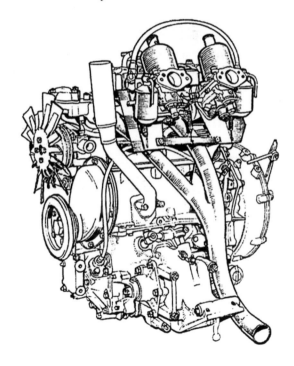

BELOW A Group 2 Competition engine made by Downton in the mid-1960s

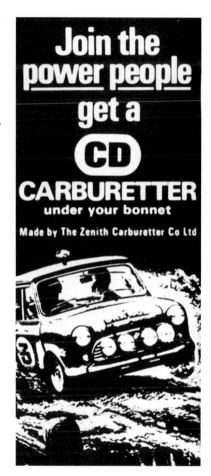

Join the power people get a CD CARBURETTER under your bonnet

Made by The Zenith Carburetter Co Ltd

And of course, you could take the other obvious route (as Cooper did) and make the engine capacity larger, either by increasing the bore size or lengthening the piston stroke, or maybe both.

Then when you had all that extra power from the engine, you could do the things to make it safely usable. You could uprate the engine mounts, the clutch, the gearbox, the suspension, the brakes, the wheels and tyres, everything from the seat you sat in and the steering wheel you twiddled to the instruments you looked at and the rubber you rode on.

You could even do it yourself if you had the spirit of adventure and a well-equipped workshop, or if you didn't mind farming the more complicated machining jobs out to the local motor engineer. And there was plenty of literature to tell you how to do it, because in parallel with the Mini tuning industry, another phenomenon grew up, of 'how-to' tuning guides and specialist magazine articles on how to make your Mini go faster, stop better, sound more sporty or handle more sharply. Just as the adage said, the more you spent, the faster you went.

Not that doing it yourself was infallible, of course. More than one would-be home-garage Mini tuner spent far too much time and money spoiling perfectly good cars, making their power delivery so peaky that they were a nightmare to drive, or in extreme cases winding up either with less power than you started with or an engine that didn't work at all.

Fortunately, for the completely technically incompetent, there was the happy medium between doing-it-yourself and having to find the cash for a Cooper – there was a whole new catalogue of people who would do all the hard work for you, or sell you straightforward modified parts that even the most modest of self-taught mechanics could safely bolt on.

Within a couple of years of the Mini being launched, there were literally dozens of them – some that justifiably disappeared without trace and others that became rightly respected, like Broadspeed, Janspeed, Longman, Oselli, Speedwell and Taurus. And the stuff they could sell you really would make a difference. Take the typical 'Stage One' tuning kit that most of them offered in one form or another. That would address the shortcomings of the carburettor and exhaust, and a mild rework-

ing of the cylinder head, but usually staying with the original valve sizes. Taurus could sell you one that in 1963 cost about £22 and trimmed a very noticeable seven and a half seconds from a standard Mini's 0-60mph time. At the higher end of the scale, in the same year, £200 spent with Speedwell could buy you an 1150cc engine with a very special alloy cylinder head (the original was cast iron), bigger valves and new valvegear, special pistons, a lightened and balanced crankshaft and flywheel assembly, and a pair of bigger SU carburettors. It would do over 105mph and 0-60mph in less than ten-and-a-half seconds, which was enough to leave even the Cooper S of the time well beaten. And the cost might have been around a third of what a complete new car could have cost you at the time, but the kit did also include new seats and additional instruments such as a rev-counter, where the original had had little more in the dashboard than the big central speedo and a fuel gauge.

But if you wanted the sharp end of Mini performance and you could pay

RIGHT Wheel arch spats soon became an essential addition to any tuned Mini

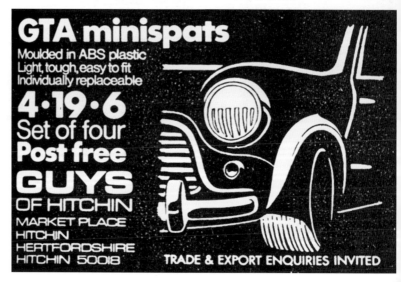

for it, the real place to go was to a little village in Wiltshire called Downton, and to the tuning firm of the same name, run by one Daniel Richmond. Already well known as a restorer of classic sports cars and preparer of racing engines, he was also, through the sport, a good friend of both Alec Issigonis and John Cooper, and when the Mini was born he wasted no time at all in making it go faster – finishing his first Mini conversion in 1959 before the car was more than a few months old.

His Downton conversions gained their industry leading reputation not only because of the power that they unlocked but because of the added refinement and reliability they could give to the car even while making it unrecognisably faster. In fact Downton,

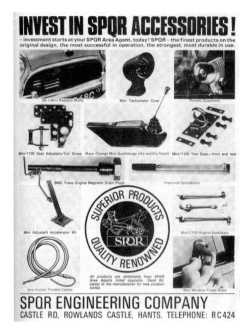

INVEST IN SPQR ACCESSORIES!

– investment starts at your SPQR Area Agent, today ! SPQR – the finest products on the original design, the most successful in operation, the strongest, most durable in use.

Mk I Mini Radiator Muffs Mini Tachometer Cowl Throttle Quadrants

Mini/1100 Seat Adjusters/Col Drops Major Change Mini Gearlinkage (the world's finest) Mini/1100 Tow Eyes–front and rear

BMC Trans Engine Magnetic Drain Plugs Improved Speedbrace

Mini Adjustafit Accelerator Kit Mini/1100 Engine Stabilisers

SUPERIOR PRODUCTS **SPQR** **QUALITY RENOWNED**

Anti-friction Throttle Cables Mini Window Finger Grips

All products are obtainable from SPQR Area Agents listed opposite. Send 6d. stamp to the manufacturer for free product leaflet.

SPQR ENGINEERING COMPANY
CASTLE RD, ROWLANDS CASTLE, HANTS. TELEPHONE: R C 424

spiced up by the likes of Radford, Hooper or Wood & Pickett had the mechanical work done by Downton.

Richmond was odd in one way, in that he was nowhere near as visible as some of the other Mini tuners, and his claims for his cars always tended to be under-rather than overstated – which you couldn't say for some. He didn't really do off-the-shelf, either; his conversions were generally done in-house, to individual order, for a remarkable customer list that at the top end included people like Sellers, Lord Snowdon, Steve McQueen, the Aga Khan – even Enzo Ferrari, who was another Mini fan. Ferrari, in fact, had known the Mini from its very earliest days, through his Grand Prix rival and fellow F1 car constructor John Cooper. In 1959 Cooper, with one of his drivers, Roy Salvadori, had taken a Mini – a prototype – to the Italian Grand Prix weekend at Monza. Ferrari's chief designer Aurelio Lampredi asked if he could try it out, disappeared with it for long

through their existing racing connections with John Cooper, had done much of the development work on the Mini Coopers, including the 'works' competition cars from Abingdon. Downton probably also built the first roadgoing Minis reliably to top 100mph, and almost anyone who went to have the bodywork and interior of their car

enough to suggest that he might have been to show it to the boss, and came back absolutely full of enthusiasm. 'If it weren't for the fact that it's so ugly', he's reported as saying, 'I'd shoot myself'.

Either way, Enzo eventually bought three Minis over the next few years, including his Downton-tuned car – which he apparently used to go and drive when he was feeling the pressures of his business and racing. He grew to be good friends with Issigonis, too; but when Issigonis offered Ferrari a Downton-tuned version of the automatic Mini when that first appeared, Ferrarri declined the offer – not because he'd gone off the Mini or even because he didn't like automatics but because he didn't feel comfortable driving right-hand-drive cars, which this one was.

As for Daniel Richmond himself, he died tragically young, in his mid-forties; but what he knew about engines, and especially Mini engines, would live on with some of the other great Mini tuners who had all started their careers with Downton - like racing preparation stars Richard Longman and Gordon Spice, and the founder of Janspeed, Jan Odor. Every one of them, like Cooper, could make the Mini special.

Chapter 10

The Wilder Bunch

ASIDE FROM THOSE RELATIVELY conventional and mostly very highly respected Mini modifiers, of course, there were some with stranger ideas of how to 'improve' the car. When it came to adding performance, most of them side-stepped subtlety and went first for the bigger engined route. You could squeeze 1293cc out of a 1275 and still stay inside the 1300cc racing class rules, so lots of people did that. And although Cooper and BMC had originally thought that 1275 was as far as the original engine could safely stretch, people started to get more by moving the centres of the cylinder bores so that they could make them even bigger (but at the expense of very marginal cooling space

between them, and the need for special crankshafts to match the new piston spacing. Then you could change the crankshaft and the height of the cylinder block to get a longer stroke, as well, until today its not at all unusual to have a 1400 or 1430cc A-Series-based Mini engine, with the even better power that that promises.

There were even wilder stretches than those, too. In the mid 1960s a Mini racer

LEFT This Autosport review of Harry Radcliffe's V8-powered Mini appeared in December, 1964

OPPOSITE Issigonis experimented with a twin-engined Mini Moke in the early 1960s

and tuner called Harry Ratcliffe, from Rochdale in Lancashire, somehow managed to squeeze a 3.5-litre Buick V8 engine into the back of the car, but still driving the front wheels! Those were bigger than usual, at 13.5 inches diameter and 6.5 inches wide to try and put down the 220bhp that the engine was producing, but the rear wheels were the standard ten-inch ones, so it looked pretty odd – but the looks weren't nearly as odd as the handling, which even Radcliffe admitted was quite scary. Worse than that, though, was that while it was very quick in a straight line, it wasn't nearly as quick around a circuit as the conventional 1300 racers.

Others had more success by sticking to less extreme transplants. Some of the best of them, for special saloon car racing where the engine didn't have to be original equipment for the car, used four-cylinder Ford engines that weren't much bigger externally than the A-

Series but offered bigger capacity and more power, and especially the overhead camshaft Ford BDA engine that was usually seen in sports racers or single-seaters.

Issigonis, meanwhile, had also experimented with another option – not one big engine but two normally sized ones, one at each end of the car, which in the first instance wasn't the now familiar Mini saloon but a new derivative, the Moke (which is described more fully in Chapter 16).

That would be introduced in 1964, but in the winter before it was launched, which was quite severe in Britain, Issigonis took a prototype of the Jeep-like Moke and turned it into something quite different. It started with the usual front-engine, front-drive layout, but

Issigonis moved the 850 engine into the back and connected it to the rear wheels, then filled the hole he'd taken it out of with a 950cc engine to drive the front wheels – not so much for performance as to create a four-wheel-drive Mini variation for the winter conditions. It worked quite well, and Issigonis apparently had a great time just playing around with it.

He also showed it to John Cooper and, maybe inevitably, that ended with the two of them setting out to build a proper twin-engined Mini each. Cooper's was ready first, with a total of 156bhp from two tuned Cooper engines, one with 81bhp the other with 76bhp, and you could change the handling characteristics of the car depending on whether you put the more powerful one in the front or the back. Sir John Whitmore, the championship-winning Mini race driver, tested the car at Brands Hatch and persuaded the competition department to build an even more powerful

version, with two Downton-tuned engines and around 175bhp, for the Targa Florio road race. And they actually ran the car, but although it was quick they couldn't keep both engines cool, so it didn't achieve much.

By then, Issigonis had completed his version, which was a lot less powerful

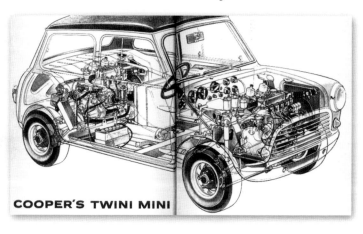

COOPER'S TWINI MINI

than Cooper's, with about 110bhp, but in some ways more complicated. The rear engine was where the back seat should be, the fuel tank was in the boot, and there were two of most things, including starter buttons and each instrument. There were also two

ABOVE This line drawing shows the twin-engined Twini Mini

gearlevers, but linked to work together – which was one of the big challenges of the layout. Issigonis called it the Mini Toucan (pronounced Two Can), and it would do 110mph, but it was another experiment that didn't handle like a Mini.

It was better behaved than Cooper's Twini-Mini, though, which almost killed him when he had a massive accident on the Kingston by-pass near his Surrey workshops after one or other of the two engines apparently failed and threw the car off the road. As Cooper fought for his life, the BMC bosses banned any further experiments with the cars. Oddly, though, a private builder had maybe got closer than either Cooper or Issigonis to making the idea work properly and he was yet another racing man, Paul Emery. A rival to Cooper in the early days of the old 500cc Formula 3, Emery created a twin-engined Mini that was completely standard at the front and used a complete Mini engine and suspension sub-frame assembly at the rear, with the steering arms locked to provide a 'normal' rear end – although Issigonis had wanted his to steer slightly. Emery also contrived linked gearshifts, and planned racing, road and special-bodied sports car versions, but never had the resources or the money to put any of his ideas properly into production. All the twin-engined Mini experiments, though, showed how the car enthused people.

It even appealed to more than one future world champion racing driver during the early stages of their careers. Britain's James Hunt came from a fairly well-off background but having flunked any real academic career he had an ambition to be a racing driver, but almost no money of his own. So with what money he earned by working as a labourer, a night porter in a hospital, a shelf-stacker in a supermarket and a van driver for the civil service, he built his own racing Mini in the family garage.

He wasn't allowed to start the first race he entered, at Snetterton, because the car didn't have a windscreen, and he never made it work properly – but he did use the money he sold it for to provide most of the deposit for the Formula Ford car that really started his racing career.

Hunt's arch-rival from the 1970s Grand Prix circus, Niki Lauda, once raced his own Mini, too. After owning a couple of Beetles he was trying the car out one night in Vienna, hit a patch of ice and crashed it. The car was for sale, but the owner (the father of the boy who had suggested Lauda should drive it) didn't know they had borrowed it. Without telling the owner about this minor problem, Lauda went to his wealthy grandmothers' house, woke her up, and borrowed enough money to buy the car – a 1275 Cooper S. And once he'd repaired it (finding the funds by selling his latest Beetle), he traded it in for another, engineless Cooper S from another Austrian racing driver, Fritz Baumgartner. He acquired an engine for it, promised his parents he had no intentions of going racing, and entered the car into his first race in April 1964, finishing second.

Having heard about that and told him again that he was banned from racing, his parents found out that he had raced the Mini again a couple of weeks later, in a local hillclimb, winning his class. His father was very angry, Niki left home, and didn't mend the rift for many years. He also traded in the Mini towards a Porsche, but another future world champion had also started his career in Issigonis's small masterpiece.

OPPOSITE Niki Lauda raced a Mini in the early 1960s

Chapter 11

Rallying Round

WHILE THE MINI MAY HAVE had a spectacularly successful career on the race tracks, some of its most famous victories of all came in what might have seemed like an even less likely branch of motor sport for such a small car – at the very top of the tree in world championship rallying.

It was probably John Handley, later turned circuit racer, who gave the Mini its first-ever competitive outing, after buying his local dealer's demonstrator car on the day of the Mini launch. He took it straight to a meeting of his local motor club, told them (to their great amusement) that he was going to rally it, and a couple of weeks later did just that, in the Worcestershire Rally, where the Mini was by no means disgraced.

At about the same time in another minor event in Lancashire, Pat Moss (sister of Stirling) and one Stuart Turner (soon to be the Mini works

ABOVE Paddy Hopkirk's Cooper S on the 1964 Monte Carlo rally

OPPOSITE Tommy Wisdom's Mini 850 at the 1960 Monte Carlo rally

team's hugely successful manager) also gave the Mini a rally outing, but complained that the car was too slow and too uncomfortable.

But as early as September 1959, barely a month after the Mini was launched, the BMC Competitions department at Abingdon showed they were at least thinking about a future role for the Mini alongside their big rally cars like the Austin Healey, with the car's first international event!

That was in the Viking Rally in Norway, where then competition manager Marcus Chamber took a virtually standard production Mini (in fact one of the first ever built) and (while supposedly acting as a support vehicle for Pat Moss's Austin A40) overcame horrible conditions to finish in 51st place. And that made them look more closely at the Mini's potential.

ABOVE Paddy Hopkirk at a rather messy looking fuel stop during the 1964 Monte Carlo rally

early problem of oil leaking onto their clutches. Still only a couple of months after its launch, though, the Mini was already becoming a regular rally competitor, and in December Nancy Mitchell and Peter Riley finished 54th and 64th overall in Portugal – preparing for the Mini's biggest test so far.

That would be in January 1960, when the Mini made its first appearance in the best known rally of all, the Monte Carlo. And it was a remarkable assault, with no fewer than six works-entered cars and six more private entries. As they always did at the time, the works team entered both male and female crews, but only the male-crewed cars survived into the final stages of the event. Driven by Peter Riley, Don Morley, Tommy Wisdom and Alec Pitts, they finished 23rd, 33rd, 55th and 73rd respectively, but they had found it very hard work.

A couple of months later, in April, Morley gave the Mini its first interna-

They made a more serious international outing in November, on Britain's RAC Rally, where a three-car team of Minis were competing in their own right rather than supposedly supporting someone else. It wasn't a very promising showing: the event itself was turned to chaos by winter weather but all three Minis had already gone out, with that

tional class win, in the Geneva Rally, while Patricia 'Tish' Ozanne was second in class. And in May 1962 it was another of the lady drivers, Pat Moss, driving one of the new 997cc Mini Coopers, who gave the Mini its first outright rally win, in the Tulip Rally in Holland. Just as it was doing on the race tracks, it was beating the traditional, big rally cars with its unique combination of talents – not much power compared to cars like the Big Healeys but not much weight either, and that amazing handling. And thanks to John Cooper, they were addressing the lack of power, too.

Through 1962 and the first half of 1963 they relied on the 997 Cooper, and then adopted the 1071 Cooper S, which

BELOW The Mini was a perfect car for rallying

was quick enough for the Minis now to be chasing outright rather than class wins – but they could hardly have expected the next big win to be as big as it was.

In 1964, the Monte was one of the blue chip headline grabbers of the motor sport calendar. Right up there, in its hey-day, with any Grand Prix, or Indianapolis or Le Mans – and arguably more glamorous than any of them, for no better reason than the magical setting of the showdown in fairytale Monte Carlo. Back then, in deep mid-winter, several hundred crews in the wildest variety of cars – some professionally prepared for

BELOW The front-wheel-drive Mini was ideal for the mountain sections of the Monte Carlo rally

the rigours of the sport, others with not much more than a book of maps and a nice warm flask of coffee – set off from points all around Europe to converge on a common starting point for the truly competitive bit, in Reims, followed by a couple of days and nights of special stages in the icy mountains above the Principality, and a final day hammering around the famous Monaco Grand Prix circuit to decide who'd won.

Mini driver Paddy Hopkirk and co-driver Henry Liddon hardly took the easy option, by choosing a starting point way behind what was then the Iron Curtain, in Minsk. But the BMC management clearly thought driving a stripped out, rally prepared Mini from Russia to the Cote d'Azure in January would be very good publicity – which then as now was really the main object of the exercise. And it apparently didn't deter them to know that they faced temperatures so low in Minsk (the startline figure was −26 degrees) that most cars had to be tow started; that they faced roads (if you could find them in the snow) that normally saw far more tractors and tanks than rally cars; or that

they faced unreadable road signs, almost non-existent daylight, minimal map detail and maximum en-route bureaucracy at border crossings (although the hosts had been very hospitable indeed at the pre-start gathering). And they had to watch their steps in other ways, too,

RIGHT Timo Makinen (right) and his co-driver Paul Easter hold up their trophy after winning the 1965 Monte Carlo Rally

because someone else was always watching them! In fact Hopkirk's first drama came before he was even out of Russia when he did nothing worse than take a wrong turn down an unmarked road - but threw the car into a 180 degree spin when he realised that the fur hat in the snow in front of them was actually holding a gun. . .

It was a gendarme rather than a soldier who stopped them the second time, deep into France when they were driving, none too slowly, down an urban one-way street, the wrong way. Road penalties in those days meant rally time penalties, and a big enough offence — which this probably was – could mean disqualification. When the gendarme asked for the crew's official rally log book to record the digression, Hopkirk explained that they were going so quickly in the wrong direction because

ABOVE Timo Makinen drives his Mini into the Aerial Hotel, London, after being disqualified from the 1966 Monte Carlo rally

he had just been informed that his mother had died and he was rushing home for the funeral, no longer in the rally at all. So that was OK, and so, of course, was Mrs Hopkirk, had the policeman bothered to check. . .

They arrived at Reims without penalties, to a jolly reception with excellent champagne and dodgy food - which caused some other crews to make additional service halts the next day, on the competitive run-in through the mountains to Monte. That 1400km 'common route' included five timed 'special stages', totalling around 132km and taking in 23km of the Col de Turini as the final stage, before the set-piece finale.

The contest, amazingly, was between the new front-drive 1071cc Cooper Ss and the big 4.7-litre rear-drive Ford Falcons – works teams head to head in a classic David and Goliath face-off. Goliath won the weigh-in and all the opening rounds, as the fearless Bo Ljungfeldt set fastest times with his Falcon on every stage. And it's worth noting just how scary Ljungfeldt was, even to a team mate like F1 world champion Graham Hill, who was never notably nervy. Later he told of following Bo over a stage and watching him pass other cars by throwing the Falcon up the face of the rocks bordering the road, then dropping back down. 'I saw him do it time after time', said Hill, 'and I still don't believe it. . .'

Paddy and Henry had the measure of the flying Falcon, though. They'd run it (and Eric Carlsson's spectacular Saab) close on every stage, and around the streets of Monte Carlo, helped by a handicapping system that levelled the playing field slightly, they did just enough to win, by the narrowest points decision. Paddy says a French journalist told him they'd done it, and he wasn't sure whether to believe him – but it was real enough when Princess Grace handed over the biggest of the half dozen trophies they'd won. Mini also won the team prize, with Timo Makinen and Rauno Aaltonen backing up. After it all, Hopkirk, Liddon and 33 EJB, the winning car, were whisked back to London to appear on the stage of Sunday Night at the London Palladium. Mini winning its first Monte really was that big a story – but it was really only the beginning.

They won the Monte again in 1965, in blizzard conditions, thanks to

Scandinavian star Makinen. And Aaltonen added a third Monte win in 1967 after a huge battle with Ove Anderson in a Lancia.

They had also 'won' in 1966, but the French organisers found a detail in the newly revised rules that let them exclude the Minis, which had actually finished 1-2-3 in one of their greatest performances ever. Having found no other technical infringements on the cars they argued that their combination of headlights and spotlights contravened the regulations, and they threw out all three cars. They also excluded all the British Ford Cortinas – so a French Citroen became the winner. . .

Convincing as it had been, though, the subsequent 1967 win was the Mini's swansong in rallying's blue-riband event as a new generation of more powerful sportscar based rivals took over at the front. Its last significant result was a near miss, when Hopkirk finished second in the 1970 Scottish Rally – but after that there were no more works rally Minis, although private entrants continued to fly the flag for quite a while. By any standards, it had been a spectacular career for such a small car.

OPPOSITE Rauno Aaltonen and Tony Ambrose after winning the 1965 RAC rally

Chapter 12

On the Road Again

WHILE ALL THIS SOCIAL CLIMBING and high-speed giant-killing had been going on, the roadgoing Mini had also been going places – developing quickly from the original car to offer more and more variations, a bit more refinement, and a few more creature comforts. But the Mini gradually lost some of its simplicity, too, so it didn't please all the people all the time.

By the mid 1960s, when the Mini was just passing its first million sales, the Swinging Sixties were in full swing and the British economy had enjoyed at least a brief period in considerably better shape than it had been in at the end of the 1950s when the Mini was conceived – not that that was going to last for long.

Society had moved on a bit, too, and while there was still the same old conservatism in the older middle and upper classes there was also a booming new youth culture, summed up by psychedelic music and Carnaby Street fashion. There was a new feeling of freedom, too, with the coming of The Pill, the end of compulsory military service, and a new wave of modern theatre with plays like Saturday Night and Sunday Morning,

Billy Liar, and Look Back in Anger. The whole society was more 'permissive', and it was a lot more adventurous. And the Mini was still right there in the heart of the social scene. In fact it had even started to spread its wings, with the first completely new variant.

That was the first Mini estate car, which was launched in September 1960 - and depending on whether you bought the Austin or the Morris version it was called the Mini Countryman or the Mini Traveller. But whatever it was called, either version was the classic British estate car, down-sized, but retaining the traditional half-timbered sides.

The Mini was reflecting the more prosperous and up-beat trend in the economy, too, and where the original was stripped of anything at all that it

LEFT By the mid-1960s Britain was enjoying an economic revival and Carnaby Street was setting the tone for fashion and music

BELOW The Morris Mini Traveller appeared in 1960 and gave the Mini extra practicality and style.

didn't need, successive versions grew ever more elaborate.

As we've seen, the first Cooper was introduced in 1961, adding performance to the menu; but the Mini was now moving on in other directions, too. The first sign that it was moving up-market also hit the road in September 1961, with the Super versions - which added oil and water gauges where the original had just had its big central speedometer and a petrol gauge, and ignition key starting, where the original had had the distinctive starter button on the floor of the car. And even more plainly aimed at a more comfort-oriented audience, a month or so later they launched the 'up-market' Wolseley Hornet and Riley Elf – Minis disguised with more exotic badges, false radiator grilles and added-on boots, which did give a bit more luggage space but completely destroyed the

Mini's simple, classless, form-follows-function looks.

In 1962, turning their backs on the old-fashioned 'Seven' name in this new youth-centred culture, they re-badged the Austin version as plain Austin Mini. But they did put more emphasis on the comfort aspects that were evolving, by replacing the De Luxe and Super versions with one car, the Super de Luxe. At much the same time, the Riley and Elf

models (which were obviously heavier) were improved by a pair of MkII versions which used a single-carburettor version of the bigger 998cc engine that would be used in twin-carb form in the Cooper from 1964.

Remarkably, too, although it was moving more up-market, in 1962 (and in real terms, not just index-adjusted), the Mini actually became cheaper than when it was launched. It wasn't about manufacturing

costs, it was about a tax cut, in the April budget, which brought the price of a basic car down from £526 to just under £496. Even more amazingly, the price dropped again in November, when purchase tax on cars was halved – while the government tried to boost the economy and control imports.

And while we're talking about Mini prices, it's worth a mention of what was surely a very strange situation for the people who built the car – and who didn't seem to have a clue as to what it should really cost. Which meant that even when they were selling Minis as quickly as they could build them, they found it very difficult to make a profit on the car.

The fact was, it was underpriced, because although it was a small car and priced as such, in engineering terms it was a complicated one, and much more expensive to build than a simple rival like the new Ford Anglia. And the problem was in the way that BMC, as it was then, worked out their prices. Put simply, they looked at what their nearest rivals cost in the showroom, and they tried as nearly as possible to match or beat them. And while that might have worked when the cars were all very similar, like the Minor and the Popular, for example, it fell down rather when production costs were as high as they were with the Mini.

In fact when the Mini first appeared, Ford (perhaps even looking to see if they could offer a response to the Mini) took one away and totally de-constructed it – not only to the last nut and bolt but to the last chassis spot weld, and costed every single component and process. It was their opinion that even with the healthy production volumes the Mini eventually reached, they couldn't have built the car for what BMC was selling it for. In their

opinion, at the original £497 BMC must have been losing £30 a car!

Ford's pricing structure, in contrast, was based on costing the materials and

build process to the penny, cutting that to the bone, and then building in a measure of profit to arrive at the showroom price. BMC, on the other hand, insisted that, using their own accounting methods and with the way they

ABOVE The Mini Clubman estate was an update of the Traveller concept, but the stick-on fake wood didn't fool anyone!

ABOVE The Mini Clubman of 1969 was an attempt to update the Mini's looks with a longer, more angular front end

album, Please Please Me, as President John F Kennedy was assassinated and as Christine Keeler and the Profumo affair threatened to bring down the British government. It was a failing economy that really pushed out the Tories, though, and brought a Labour government and Harold Wilson to Number 10 Downing Street in October 1964 – with his Chancellor's first budget, a month later, putting tax up again to try and stop the pound's downhill slide.

In May 1965 the Mini added a version to appeal to a whole different spread of drivers, with the first automatic gearbox option. In 1966, England's footballers won the World Cup and Britain introduced the 70mph speed limit – as well as wage and price freezes and borrowing restrictions to try to get runaway inflation, and unemployment, back under control. But for the moment, the Mini was still holding on to its sales success.

And inevitably given the way the motor industry works, there was soon a more seriously updated new model range, which appeared in 1967 (when production was almost a quarter of a million cars) as the Mini MkII (or the Elf and Hornet MkIII). The MkII continued the move up-market, with a

shared out the overall company overheads to include the Mini, the car was always profitable. It was very hard to judge.

Either way, by the early 1960s it was clearly around to stay. The 970, 1071 and 1275 Coopers all arrived as the 1960s were getting into their swing, as the Beatles had recorded their first

larger rear window (which did improve rearward visibility), a bigger grille and new badges (which were purely cosmetic), better seats and improved interior trim (which were good but at the slight expense of some of the Mini's original interior oddment space), and bigger, more easily visible rear lights (which did look more modern). A bigger-engined version of the mainstream car appeared, too, in saloon and estate versions as the Mini 1000 Super de Luxe – and you could now even have the 998cc engine in the workhorse van and pick-up variants. Arguably most important of all, the Cooper gained the Mini's first all-syncromesh gearbox, which would be available across the range a year later.

BELOW Even Beatle George Harrison loved Minis

ABOVE The 1275GT replaced the Cooper but lacked real zest

There were recurring signs in the wider world, too, of the kind of problems that had brought the Mini into the world in the first place – with the stirrings of a new oil crisis. Again the con-

flict was in the middle east, this time the Six-Day War, but again the fear was that Europe's oil and fuel supplies would be threatened, so the small car was in focus again. At home in Britain, too, the economy was in serious trouble, to the extent that the pound was devalued by 14.3 per cent in November 1967, with the obvious effect of making imports more expensive, and that, too, included oil, so fuel prices started to shoot up.

In the Spring Budget in 1968 taxes were raised again, and so was petrol duty, but the Mini was as well placed as any small car to survive, maybe even capitalise on that. So Mini sales kept growing, and in spite of all the external problems, every year from 1968 to 1971 saw record sales. It also continued its gentrification, and in some ways its drift from the purity of Issigonis's original packaging. The new all-synchro gearboxes were unarguably a good thing, and a lot of people probably felt more comfortable with proper door handles instead of the original string pulls, and with wind-up windows instead of the original sliding glass – but those were the sort of refinements you could only have at the expense of some of the original interior storage space, like the huge front door pockets. They even took away one of the Mini's original styling signatures, when they replaced the exterior door hinges with concealed ones. Which may have made the Mini look more con-

ventional, but it didn't make it better.

They took the cosmetic changes another step further (some would say a step too far) with the bluff-nosed Clubman in 1969, and that further compromised the interior space with bigger seats, a more or less full dashboard (again at the expense of oddment space) and more trim. The up-spec Mini 1000 replaced the MkII Super de Luxe, and misguidedly thinking they were offering a cut-price alternative to the Coopers, British Leyland (as it had become) launched the 1275GT, which had the long-nosed Clubman-style shape, 'Rostyle' steel wheels pretending to be sporty alloys, and a not very potent single-carb version of the 1275 engine.

With just 60bhp compared to the earlier 1275S's 76bhp, it wasn't as sporty as it thought it was, but it was cheaper to build than the Coopers, and BL didn't have to pay the £2 per car royalty they had always payed to John Cooper for the use of his name. In July 1971 new boss Donald Stokes would pull the plug on the Cooper deal, and (for now) the Mini Cooper name would be no more. Which went to show how little the latest management understood what the market really wanted.

Chapter 13

Into the Future

ALEC ISSIGONIS HAD BEEN knighted in August 1969, exactly a decade after his greatest creation had been launched, and he went to Buckingham Palace in a Mini Cooper. But most of the news wasn't as positive as that. The 1970s started as the 1960s had finished, with Britain in political turmoil and economic downturn, and further threats to world oil supplies, and petrol prices, in the wake of continuing middle east unrest.

Total Mini production had just passed its second million in 1969, though, and would pass its third in 1972, which shows how well it had held up for almost thirteen years – long after almost any other car would long ago have been replaced by something more 'modern', or more appealing to a fickle market. You could argue that that was at least partly because in real terms the Mini was never cheaper than in the early 1970s. In fact adjusted to 1959 values, the cost of a basic Mini in 1973 would have been just £370, compared to an actual 1959 launch price of £497. But whatever else the Mini had done it had

The bonus, though, was that there were no more huge development costs for the new versions as they evolved, just the sort of investment any car maker would put into any facelifted model, and the Mini, although no longer setting records, was selling well enough to earn its keep.

That really now meant, though, that the Mini was marking time rather than changing significantly. It had been through the 'chic' phase, and if you wanted to make a style statement now you were more likely to do it with something big like the newly launched Range Rover rather than something small like the old Mini. So whenever there was anything new in Mini-world over the next generations it tended to be either in the form of a 'special edition', or to satisfy increasingly strict regulations.

To be fair, they did keep the Mini reasonably up to date with new technologies as they came onto the parts shelves via newer cars in the group, and they did steadily improve the things that

also genuinely risen above that traditional short life-cycle, and really it was still only at the beginning.

Having said that, its annual production figure had already passed its peak by the time the three-millionth car was built, and although the original Mini, amazingly, still had almost thirty years to run, it would never again approach the numbers it sold in that first decade and a bit.

needed improving. So troublesome bits like gearboxes and driveshaft joints were beefed up, alternators replaced dynamos in 1973, inertia-reel seat belts were offered, and you could have both a laminated windscreen and Dunlop Denovo 'run-flat' tyres (on 12-inch wheels) on the 1275GT by 1972. And they kept fiddling with the small things to keep the Mini 'fresh', and as ever to make it seem more up-market. So the 1970s were the decade of stripy seat materials, tinted glass, new grilles, bumpers and wheelarches, locking petrol caps and reversing lamps. In 1974 the basic 850 Mini even gained a heater as standard – amazingly, for the very first time!

The economic situation was still pretty desperate as Britain faced industrial unrest, the three-day working week because of power cuts, and another change of government. And car owners were suffering as badly as anybody.

Between January 1974 and January 1975 the price of petrol virtually doubled, and for the first time ever 25 per cent inflation helped push the price of a new Mini past £1000 in 1975. Industrial problems were so bad that British Leyland itself was taken into government ownership and the start of a long period of near extinction.

So the Mini was obviously having to fight for its future alongside newer rivals, and with no chance of major changes the only way it could do it was with minor ones, and a bit of new window-dressing.

In 1976 that brought options like a heated rear window, hazard lights, face-level ventilation, and radial tyres for all models. In 1977 it was a dipping interior mirror, reclining seats for more models, new trim and new steering wheels. And 1975 had seen the first of the 'special editions' – the Mini 1000 Special, which had coachlined green and white paint, reclining seats with bright orange striped upholstery, special carpets and chromed door mirrors. In 1979, with inflation apparently coming under control and the Mini in real

ABOVE The Countryman struggled on to the end of the 1970s. This 1979 example has fashionable stick-on stripes in place of the fake wood

terms back at close to 1959 levels, you could celebrate Mini's twentieth anniversary (or possibly the birth of the Thatcher years) with the Mini 1100 LE - another special edition, with metallic silver or rose paint, a vinyl roof, door stripes, tartan trim and special instruments. Even the Mini van had improved trim options, and in the late 1970s it was still Britain's best-selling small van.

But total annual sales were now below 200,000 and falling fast and within a couple of years they would be below 70,000 a year. Still they kept doing what they could afford to keep the Mini up to

ABOVE The Mini Metro was unveiled in 1980 as Britain's new small car, but the Mini went on to outlast it

subsequent model and special edition names included Chelsea, Piccadilly, Ritz and Designer; Advantage had a tennis theme; and Sprite, Red Hot and Jet Black were meant to mean sporty.

One thing the Mini did do in the early 1980s was to survive the launch of the Mini Metro, which was supposed to have been the Mini's successor and in fact by 1983 had become Britain's best selling car, while Mini production had fallen even further, to less than 50,000 cars. But there was now no economic pressure to kill it, so on it soldiered – propped up, amazingly, by a new cult following in Japan, where sales rocketed!

date, but through the 1980s that was more and more a question of hanging on rather than going forwards. One good thing at the start of the decade was the end of the Clubman and the return to the classic Mini shape as the only option. The most obvious changes for the next few years, though, were the badges: there was the City, which became the E, while HL became HLE and HLE became Mayfair – harking back to the early 1960s street-chic heyday. And in similar vein,

Sir Alec Issigonis, sadly, didn't survive the 1980s, and he died on 2 October 1988, after years of failing health. It meant that he missed a very entertaining Mini thirtieth birthday party at Silverstone in 1989, and something that he personally would surely have been very pleased to see – the rebirth of the Mini Cooper. That was a direct result of the birthday party, where John Cooper had showed his idea of a Cooper for the 1990s in the spirit of the original. Rover (who were now in charge) liked it too, and sanctioned an official kit to turn ordinary Minis into Coopers; and in 1990 they went the whole way and re-introduced the Mini Cooper as an official part of the range. It was an instant best seller, and through to the end of the classic Mini's life, Coopers were again the stars of the range. In 1991 the Cooper S reappeared, and almost at the end of the Mini's life there was the most powerful production Cooper of them all, the Cooper S Works – which had 90bhp, a top speed of over 100mph, and 0-62mph in less than nine seconds. It was a great celebration of the Mini at forty.

BELOW The Cooper made a welcome return in 1989. This is a 1993 1.3i

Chapter 14

An End and a Beginning

PARTLY ON THE STRENGTH OF THAT surprising new Japanese enthusiasm for the Mini, partly thanks also to the revival of the Cooper name, and due to a new taste for 'retro chic', the Mini was actually more successful in the mid 1990s than it had been through most of the 1980s, justifying one final round of engineering changes to help it meet the latest emissions and crash-test rules. And while surely nobody back in 1959, not even Issigonis, could have imagined it happening, the Mini made it into the 21st century.

In fact the last example of the classic Mini rolled off the Longbridge production line (where the first Minis had also been born) in October 2000, more than 41 years after Job One. By any standards it had been an incredible life-span for one car, but the story still wasn't over yet.

It probably would have been, of course, had it been entirely in the hands of the Mini's original makers, but now there was a new twist in the tale, that would see the Mini reborn, as the new MINI. And that was BMW.

That's getting slightly ahead of the story, though, so go back for a moment to the 1960s, when, amazingly, Issigonis and BMC were already looking at a potential replacement for the original Mini!

Even by that time, really small cars other than the Mini had generally grown a bit bigger, and a bit less basic – so that was the direction they thought they had to go down. Almost from the start they had toyed with the idea of stretched and widened versions of the real thing, usually with more trim and equipment, but none of those got beyond the thinking about it stage. In the 1960s, though, Issigonis produced a design study labelled simply 9X, for a slightly bigger car to replace the Mini. It had the same transverse engine/front-drive layout and the same wheel-at-each-corner packaging for maximum space utilisation, but it was a boxier shape, just as roomy and on a longer wheelbase but thanks to almost no overhangs even shorter overall.

It would have been lighter, too, and simpler to build, and it would have had a modern overhead camshaft engine, but as BMC became BMH and BMH became British Leyland it was quietly forgotten after just two prototypes had been built. With Issigonis nearing retirement, it was also his last complete project, but obviously not one to be remembered by.

There were other ideas from other directions. Project ADO74 was started in 1972 and would have been a bit bigger than the real Mini but it was another victim of the company changes. And its cousin ADO88, started in 1973, which shared much of ADO74's underpinnings, for potential economy of scale, didn't survive itself but evolved through the slightly larger LC8 study to become the Metro, as launched in 1980. But contrary to earlier plans, the Mini Metro wasn't now a Mini replacement, it was a new, slightly larger model to run in parallel with the original. A little later, in the early 1990s, there would also

OPPOSITE The 9X was an early concept for a replacement Mini which Issigonis himself was involved in

BELOW The Minki was an experiment in fitting a Mini with a modern K-series engine

ABOVE AD074 was a still-born Mini replacement of the early 1970s

CENTRE AD088 had hints of of the Metro in its styling

be other exercises like the cars called Minki One and Minki Two, which aimed to produce what the Mini might have been had it been designed thirty-odd years later. Both had Mini looks, both used variations of the excellent, modern Rover K-Series engine, Minki Two with the usual four cylinders, Minki One chopped down to three. But like the other 'replacement' projects, that was as far as they went.

And that was really the story of the classic Mini from here on until the end of its production life – they more or less always thought that they wanted to replace it, but could never quite find the way or why to do it.

But now go back to the 1990s, when everything changed again, for what had now become the Rover Group. For a while, Rover had had a partnership with Honda, and Honda thought they had a partnership that was going to last a lot longer, but early in 1994 German car giant BMW came onto the scene and in effect bought Rover from under Honda's noses, from British Aerospace who had in turn bought Rover for next to nothing, from the British government who had been bailing it out for so long.

From most angles it looked like a strange move for the highly successful Bavarian premium car maker to take over the struggling 'English patient' as

ABOVE Bernd Pischetsrieder, BMW's Rover boss, was one of the men behind the new MINI

the premium sporty saloon market, a new Mini would give the opportunity of the big expansion BMW needed if it was ever to move beyond being a mid-sized, specialist manufacturer. So the stage was set – BMW would build a new generation Mini, much smaller and cheaper than anything with a BMW badge, and to distinguish it from the 'classic' Mini while still taking advantage of the heritage, they would call it MINI.

Being in effect a different brand within the group (as Rolls-Royce was also about to be at the other end of the market), the MINI wouldn't have to follow the BMW norm of having rear-wheel drive – in fact it was a positive virtue that it should carry on with front drive, as a defining point. BMW, too, saw it commercially in a way that Rover never had, not just as one MINI, but as the start of a whole new MINI family of variations, and a brand that eventually might sell 500,000 cars a year in its own right. Which put an entirely different complexion on the matter.

some of their own directors came to call Rover – but what they had really bought was an inroad into Land Rover technology to support their own future 4x4 plans, and some interesting badges, including Austin-Healey, Riley and MG – and not least Mini. And although BMW had no wish to continue building original Minis forever, they did have a corporate intent to build 'premium' cars in every market segment they chose to enter – and that included the sub-compact Mini segment.

Alongside their other plans, to enter niches like 4x4 and the smaller end of

So by 1995, creating the new MINI was a serious project for the BMW and Rover engineers and designers, and that same year BMW's man in charge of Rover, Bernd Pischetsrieder (who incidentally was related to Alec Issigonis through Alec's mother's family) confirmed to the motoring press that the project was progressing – if not very quickly. At the time he didn't expect it to be launched for another four or five years. And he expected Rover to play as large a part in creating the new car as BMW, 'because the British understand that sort of car better than anyone else'.

In normal industry fashion, there were in fact several competing projects running in parallel, each hoping to be given the final go-ahead. BMW's earlier small car studies like the electric-powered sub-compact E1 and the radical rear-engined three-seater Z13 really didn't have much relevance to the MINI programme though. And as it turned out, neither did two later exercises from Rover, Spiritual and Spiritual Too, futuristic hatches created under Rover's highly respected design chief Geoff Upex.

Those were unveiled in March 1997 at the Geneva Motor Show and had a lot of innovative engineering – including three-cylinder engines mounted longitudinally under the rear seats and driving the rear wheels, exceptionally light weight, Hydragas suspension and a huge amount of interior space for the

BELOW The Spiritual was one concept of what the new Mini should look like

external size, just like the real thing. Spiritual was a three-door hatch, Spiritual Too was a longer five-door, and both carried MINI badges, which led a lot of people to think that they were a real clue to how the new MINI would be, but they were really just another blind alley. In fact another show car, ACV30, which had appeared a couple of months earlier, in January 1997 to celebrate the Mini's final Monte Carlo Rally win, was in some ways a much better indicator of where next generation MINI thinking was heading.

The label stood for Anniversary Concept Vehicle 30, and the tube-framed, rear-engined MGF-powered two-seater was painted in classic Cooper red and white livery. And looking back on it now, you can see hints of MINI outside, and especially inside. It was no more really the new MINI than any of the others, though.

But the project that actually would in time become the new MINI, internally known as E50, was already well under way, and by 1996 it had been handed over to Rover to turn it into the real car.

ABOVE The stunning ACV 30 of 1997 was built to celebrate Mini's Monte Carlo successes and gave some hints as to what the new Mini would be like

Chapter 15

A Legend Turns 50…

WHAT IS IT ABOUT THE MINI THAT endeared it to millions of admirers around the world? The Mini succeeded where others had failed in providing comfortable, reliable transportation in a small package… it also looked good and was fun to drive!

It was a bestseller in the small car market and didn't really face any serious opposition until Hillman launched

their Imp in 1963. Even then, the Mini was a more frequent sight on the road than its rival and continued to dominate the market even after Vauxhall introduced their Chevette in 1975. Despite being more modern and more practical, the Chevette failed to usurp the Mini which continued its popularity even after the launch of the Metro in 1980.

Although the Metro never actually replaced the Mini, production figures dipped during the 1980s and interest in the now-iconic design was not revived until the re-introduction of the famous Mini Cooper in 1989. This helped the car retain its desirability and driver appeal throughout the 1990s, right up to the end of production on 4 October 2000. Nine years after its demise, the Mini is still a common sight on Britain's roads, and the surviving pre-1980s models in particular are now

widely regarded as collectors items. Indeed, such is the high regard in which the first Minis are held, they have their own enthusiasts club. The 1959 Mini Register boasts a total of almost 100 cars manufactured in the first year of production that are still in existence 50 years on.

As 2009 approached, MINI enthusiasts all over the world looked to BMW in anticipation of a model that celebrated the car's 50th birthday. But, at the time of writing, nothing had officially been announced despite much speculation. There had, after all, been special models that commemorated the MINI's 20th, 30th and 40th anniversaries whilst BMW had already pro-

duced the MINI 7, Checkmate and Park Lane. So, whilst the world waited with baited breath, prospective owners had to make do with the MINI One MkII launched in 2007 with the Clubman arriving the following year and a convertible option offered from 2009.

At a first glance the MINI One MkII appears almost identical to its predecessor but every single body panel of the new machine has been changed – in most cases to accommodate the ever more stringent safety requirements demanded by Euro NCAP and their transatlantic cousins at the NHTSA. Its front end has been slightly raised and the overall length of the vehicle has increased by 60mm to 3,699mm.

LEFT TO RIGHT
Frank Stephenson's early concepts for the MINI are surprisingly similar to the car we know today

Internally, tribute is paid to the Issigonis pen by way of the huge centrally mounted speedometer which now incorporates not only the fuel gauge but also the radio and the optional satellite navigation system. Twenty-first century technology even filters its way down to the simple matter of getting in and out and starting the engine – the traditional key having been replaced by a proximity

BELOW The new MINI MkII interior

ABOVE Producing a full-sized 'clay' of the new MINI

key which automatically unlocks the doors when you approach the car and allows the driver to fire up the engine with just the simple press of a dash-mounted button. The MINI's famous rear-seat roominess – or lack of it – has been tackled with TARDIS-like ingenu-ity by sculpting away the backs of the front seats. However, for all of the clever styling and increased safety, perhaps the most significant changes are to be found hidden under the bonnet.

The basic MINI One is powered by an all new 1.4-litre 16-valve four-cylinder

motor designed jointly by BMW and PSA Peugeot Citroën – the Prince I4 – which produces a healthy 95bhp and offers a top speed of 115mph and acceleration to 62mph in a shade less than 11 seconds. More exciting is the development of the Cooper designated models.

The standard Cooper now benefits from a 1.6-litre derivative of the Prince I4 fitted with BMW's Valvetronic variable timing system and a direct-shift six-speed box. The Cooper's hi-tech goodies combine to offer 120bhp and, for those with a heavy right foot, a top

speed of 126mph and 0-62mph in just 9.1 seconds whilst offering an improvement in fuel economy over its predecessor by an incredible 19%.

For those in need of an even quicker motoring fix, there is the Cooper S. Once more it is the superlative 1.6-litre 16-valve BMW/PSA Prince I4 that is pressed into action but, whereas the MkI received its muscle boosting steroid injection by way of a supercharger, the MkII makes use of a twin-scroll turbocharger; a clever innovation used for the first time in a car of this class, it reduces exhaust gas counter-pressure when the engine is running at lower speeds and offers increased power and thrust on less fuel than a normal tur-

OPPOSITE The MINI is built at a state of the art plant in Oxford, England

BELOW The MINI concept car was very similar to the final production model

bocharger system. Combined with an "overboost" feature which raises torque under hard acceleration the result is an immensely powerful motor which propels the diminutive "S" from 0-62mph in 7.1 seconds on the way to a top speed in excess of 140mph whilst still offering a remarkable fuel economy of 40.9mpg.

The MINI's green credentials are further enhanced by the introduction of a 1.6-litre Peugeot DV6 powered Cooper D – the first Cooper-badged diesel in

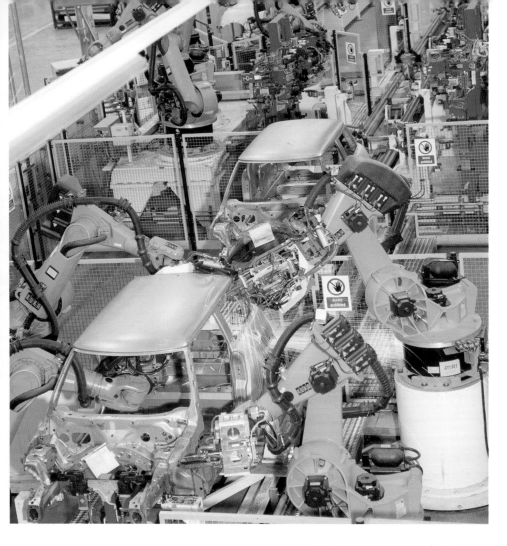

the marque's illustrious history. An oil-burner it may be, but with acceleration to 62mph in 9.9 seconds and a top speed of 121mph, there is no denying that it is a car worthy of the Cooper name. Thanks to BMW's Efficient Dynamics system which incorporates an automated engine stop-start system, the tail pipe emits just 104 g/km2 of carbon dioxide whilst returning fuel economy of 74mpg putting it in the same environmentally-conscious class as the fabled Toyota Prius hybrid.

BMW have also unveiled the first ever electric-powered MINI. Showcased at the 2008 Los Angeles Auto Show, the MINI E has been designed to adhere to new California regulations that require manufacturers to offer zero emission vehicles. Powered by an Asynchronous electric motor, the MINI E will be limited to a top speed of 95mph and have a range of between 96 to 109 miles on a single charge. It was announced that a total of 500 were being built to be trialled by California residents and such was the popularity of the idea that around 9,500 people registered their interest in leasing a MINI E at a cost of $850 per month. By leading the race for innovation, once again BMW have raised the bar and set a new class standard but, importantly, in doing so have not sacrificed the key factors that define the MINI's character.

Enthusiast clubs around the world began celebrating the Mini's 50th birthday as 2009 kicked off and events were planned throughout the year. The largest, without doubt, is the International Mini Meeting that will be held at Longbridge, Birmingham, on 7-10 August. Organised by the Birmingham Mini Owners Club, IMM 2009 promises a weekend of fun and entertainment along with the chance to enter your vehicle into competitions. Other events included: the British Mini Fair at Bingley in January; Brooklands Mini Day in March; the Mini United Festival at Silverstone and the Miniworld Riviera Run from Reading to Newquay in May. The National Mini

Show at Stanford Hall, Lutterworth is planned for September. The whole Mini community, it seems, are determined to celebrate the car's half century in style...

Chapter 16

Mini Models
Through The Years

Austin Mini Seven and Morris Mini Minor 1959

AS LAUNCHED IN AUGUST 1959, THE original Mini rewrote the small car rulebook. Its combination of transverse engine, front-wheel drive, tiny ten-inch diameter wheels and rubber-sprung suspension was unique, and the brilliant design meant that the amount of room in the car for four people was remarkable in such a compact package. Even the functional looks were just part of the Mini's huge character.

Mini Countryman Traveller 1960

BMC SOON REALISED THAT THERE was more potential in the Mini than just the saloon versions, and just as with cars like the Minor, an estate car was an obvious addition to the range. The Countryman (or Traveller) had similar passenger space but a lot more luggage room, and a style of its own with its traditional timber trim. Unlike the Elf and Hornet it looked like a real Mini, too, and it was a big winner.

Mini van/pickup
1960

ONCE THEY HAD ADDED THE rather genteel Countryman/Traveller estate versions, it was a relatively easy step to capitalise further on the new rear-end shape with workhorse versions in the shape of the Mini van (which was in effect an estate without rear seats and windows) and the pick-up, which had a short, two seat cabin and a surprisingly roomy open rear load area. They were another big success story.

Mini Cooper
1961

IT DIDN'T TAKE LONG FOR ENTHUSI-
astic drivers to discover that the Mini had
sensational handling and that it could
easily handle more power and performance. You could soon buy both over the
counter from aftermarket tuners, but in
1961 BMC, in partnership with racing car
constructor John Cooper, created the first
'official' go-faster Mini, with the original
997cc, 55bhp, 88mph Mini Cooper. It was
a success beyond their wildest dreams.

Riley Elf/Wolseley Hornet 1961

AS WELL AS THE AUSTIN AND MORRIS names, in the early 1960s BMC owned many other badges, including the 'up-market' Riley and Wolseley brands – and with the Elf and the Hornet they found a way to 'gentrify' the Mini. They had false bonnets and grilles, longer boots, and a bit more trim inside, including some token wood! To some people, that was really missing the point of the Mini's basic simplicity.

Mini Cooper S
1963

THE FIRST MINI COOPER S TOOK THE Cooper go-faster formula to new levels, both on road and track, and in the world of rallying. In quick succession, there were three first generation Ss, the high-revving 70bhp, 95mph 1071, the classic 76bhp, 97mph 1275, and finally the very exotic and very rare 65bhp 970 – which even more than the others was mainly aimed at motorsport. And all of them further raised the new car's profile.

33 EJB 1963

BY THE EARLY 1960S THE MINI WAS well established as a competition car, but in January 1964 33 EJB, crewed by Paddy Hopkirk and Henry Liddon, won rally-ing's biggest prize, the Monte Carlo Rally. Their 1071 Cooper S set off in freezing conditions from Minsk, and battled with far bigger rivals all the way to the final speed tests in Monte Carlo. With other Minis in fourth and seventh places, BMC also won the coveted Team Prize.

Mini Moke 1964

THE MOKE WAS DEFINITELY THE most extreme factory-built variant of the Mini, and one of the most characterful. It was a real utility vehicle with a style of its own – a cross between military-style Jeep and beach-buggy. The engine, gearbox, suspension, brakes, steering and all the other running gear was standard Mini; the body was a simple, open platform with four seats and an optional canopy – so the Moke was a car for all reasons.

A Monkee's Mini
1967

IN 1967, MIKE NESMITH FROM THE Monkees ordered a very special Mini that would soon be described as the most expensive Mini in the world. It was based on a Cooper 1275 S, tuned by Downton, with body and interior by Radford. It had special seats, instruments, radio and tape systems, and air-conditioning, because Mike planned to take the car home to America – so the price of more than £3600 didn't even include purchase tax!

Mini MkII
1967

HAVING SURVIVED ITS EARLY CRISES and become part of the culture, the Mini had to evolve without changing the basics, and the MkII continued the process, with a bigger rear window, bigger grille, bigger rear lights, better seats and more up-market interior trim. It was moving away from the original simplicity slightly, but it was what the market now wanted, and it did give them the chance to make steady mechanical improvements, too.

Mini Clubman
1969

JUST AS THEY'D DONE WITH THE Elf and Hornet, with the Clubman they tried to turn the Mini into something more than it was, or needed to be. There was no other reason for the longer, squarer, uglier nose than trying to be different – and what they misguidedly thought of as more modern and stylish. But the classic Mini's style was actually in the fact that it never was styled, it was just form following function.

Mini 1000
1969

AS THE BASIC MINI GREW A BIT more civilised it also grew heavier, and the 1000cc engine was a way to compen-sate. It also introduced supposedly more up-market features, like wind-up win-dows and concealed door hinges – losing some of the original Mini's most distinc-tive design signatures in favour of what they thought was more chic. It wasn't a bad car at all, but it was getting away from Issigonis's engineering basics.

Mini 1275 GT
1969

THE 1275 GT DIDN'T REPLACE THE Cooper S because it was a better car, it was just cheaper to build - and it avoided the £2 per car royalty to John Cooper for using his name. But it was a big mistake, because alongside the real Coopers it was very ordinary indeed. It didn't have the power, didn't have the performance, didn't have the sporty character, and with its Clubman-based long-nose body it didn't even have the looks.

Mini Cabriolet
1991

TO BE FAIR, THE CABRIOLET WAS A variant they had to try, but the Mini was no great shape for having its roof chopped off and a soft-top substituted. The Cabrio didn't look bad with the top up, but short of losing the rear seats (which was a non-starter) there was nowhere to stow the bulky top when it was lowered, so it stuck out of the back like a sore thumb – and the shell became very bendy, too.

Cooper S Works
1999

THE ORIGINAL COOPER S WORKS, in the classic Mini shape, completed the late 1990s rehabilitation of the Cooper name into the original Mini range, as first generation production headed for the end of the line. The two versions, Touring and 5 Sport were the hottest production Coopers of all, both with 90bhp 1275 engines and sub-ten second 0-60mph times, and the 5 Sport with a five-speed gearbox and 13-inch wheels.

MINI One
2001

WHEN BMW RE-INVENTED THE MINI as the MINI, they did it with a real understanding of what the Mini had been, and a genuine respect for its heritage. Without being in any way retro, the design (inside and out) screamed 'Mini!' It also lived up to the original's giant-killing reputation for decent performance and amazing handling – even in the basic MINI One's case, with 90bhp 1.6 engine it was good for 115mph. It was superbly well built, too.

MINI Cooper
2001

TO THEIR CREDIT, BMW ALSO RECOG-
nised that MINI without Cooper would
be like a party without jelly, so the Cooper
philosophy (and name) returned from
Day One, with the 115bhp 1.6-litre MINI
Cooper alongside the MINI One. Next up
was the new MINI Cooper S, with a supercharger, 163bhp, a top speed of 135mph
and 60mph in less than eight seconds. The
new 210bhp S Works offered over 140mph
and 60mph in under seven seconds.

MINI Convertible
2004

THE NEW MINI, WITH THE LARGER body which was one inevitable consequence of 21st century safety regulations, was a much better basis for a good-looking soft-top car than the original drop-top Mini had been, even with the top down. It gained easy-to-live-with open-aired versatility without losing much by way of chassis dynamics or performance, and best of all the new MINI Convertibles included Cooper versions – including the Cooper S Works, which was still a great driver's car.

MINI One MkII
2007

UPDATED FOR 2007, THE SECOND generation MINI One continues the legacy under BMW's watchful eye. Powered by a new engine built in co-operation with PSA Peugeot Citroën, it retains the basic shape of the MkI despite every body panel being completely redesigned to satisfy ever more stringent Euro-NCAP safety requirements. However, all this has been achieved without losing a single ounce of the fun-factor that makes the MINI so special to so many.

MINI Cooper D MkII 2007

WHEN THE ORIGINAL MINI WAS IN its heyday, diesel engines were still for trucks, tractors and taxis and a diesel small enough to fit in a Mini would have been a very under-powered, unrefined thing. The MINI Cooper D, the first ever oil-burner to bear the Cooper name, is a very different beast. Thanks to BMW's Efficient Dynamics system it boasts economy of 74mpg and a carbon footprint comparable to the Toyota Prius whilst still offering acceleration to 63mph in less than 10 seconds and a top speed in excess of 120mph. "Mum's Taxi" takes on a whole new meaning!

MINI Clubman
2008

INTRODUCED IN 2008, THE MINI Clubman proved to be an instant hit with its Cooper, Cooper S and Cooper D variations. Although the front (up to the B-pillar) is identical to the hatchback models, it is at this point where any similarity ends. The Clubman is 241mm longer which provides more leg room and has a larger boot, accessed by double doors. Some experts claim it is more of a Countryman or Traveller than a Clubman but BMW do not own the rights to those historic MINI names.

MINI John Cooper Works

2008

UNVEILED AT THE 2008 GENEVA Auto Show, the John Cooper Works models are available in both Hatchback and Clubman forms. Boasting a twin-scroll turbocharger, revamped transmission, BMW's Dynamic Traction Control and Dynamic Stability Control as well as four-piston disc brakes, the JCW can produce a blistering 211hp at 6,000rpm with the maximum torque reading 260Nm at 1,850-5,600rpm (280Nm with the Overboost function). This allows for a 0-62mph time of just 6.5 seconds and provides a top speed of 148mph.

The pictures in this book were provided courtesy of the following:

GETTY IMAGES
101 Bayham Street, London NW1 0AG

NATIONAL MOTOR MUSEUM TRUST
Beaulieu, Brockenhurst, Hampshire SO42 7ZN

BMW GREAT BRITAIN
Bracknell, Berkshire RG12 8TA

BRITISH MOTOR INDUSTRY HERITAGE TRUST
Gaydon, Warwickshire CV35 0BJ

CAR PHOTO LIBRARY
www.carphoto.co.uk

Creative Director Kevin Gardner

Published by Green Umbrella Publishing

Series Editors Jules Gammond and Vanessa Gardner

Written by Brian Laban with Jon Stroud, Ian and Claire Welch